"I know of no other book that deals with i
directly, and I can't imagine another book will come along to fill this void better than *Note to Self*. Pastor Joe Thorn offers a richly pastoral, theological, and practical guide for thinking through the Christian life. After reading *Note to Self*, you will not only have Joe's notes on how to preach to yourself on issues related to God, others, and yourself, but also you will also have a model for practicing the discipline on your own."

Ed Stetzer, President, LifeWay Research

"*Note to Self* is a gospel-guided smart bomb scoring a direct hit on our strongholds of emptiness. But the explosion it detonates is life giving. It clears the way for Christ to enter in with powers of salvation where we really need help."

Ray Ortlund, Lead Pastor, Immanuel Church,
Nashville, Tennessee

"I am thoroughly engrossed with Joe Thorn's personal meditations on preaching the gospel to oneself. He combines a clear biblical knowledge with an excellent grasp of doctrine from a historical Reformed perspective and is able to press home a rich application of each aspect of truth to the development of personal holiness. These applications are not trite, but arise from knowledge of the church's best soul doctors. My wife and I have been reading this each evening and have profited greatly. Each chapter can be managed in less than five minutes but provides an evening's worth of rich reflection."

Tom J. Nettles, Professor of Historical Theology,
The Southern Baptist Theological Seminary

"Martyn Lloyd-Jones once said that most of your unhappiness is due to the fact that you are listening to yourself instead of talking to yourself. Joe Thorn brings this truth to bear on a new generation in *Note to Self*. It's filled with pastoral concern and practical advice packaged as brief notes. I've been looking for a book like this my entire Christian life, and it's every bit as good as I hoped it would be. I'm buying a copy for everyone in my church."

Steve McCoy, Pastor, Doxa Fellowship; blogger,
Reformissionary

"Joe Thorn's gift to our spiritual well-being is a contemporary, practical example of what the Puritan pastor Richard Baxter called 'discursive meditation.' At once both convicting and exhilarating, *Note to Self* is a great resource for cultivating the godly habit of preaching to oneself."

C. Ben Mitchell, Graves Chair of Moral Philosophy,
Union University

"Joe Thorn has not only given us a good piece of writing, he's given us a great idea! *Note to Self* is a series of brief notes in which Joe preaches the gospel to himself on a wide range of topics. The notes offer memorable insights on our view of God, others, and self. Everyone should write 'notes to self.' Read this book and learn firsthand how to write the gospel into every nook and cranny of your life!"

> **Jonathan Dodson,** Lead Pastor, Austin City Life, Austin,
> Texas; founding leader, The GCM Collective; author,
> *Gospel-Centered Discipleship*

"Joe Thorn is my favorite kind of pastor—a theologian and a shepherd. Even better, he is a serious follower of Jesus Christ. Listen to him 'talk to himself' and you will discover that he is doing more listening than talking. Read *Note to Self* and it will help you to hear God's Word and discern the gracious moving of his Spirit in your own life."

> **John Koessler,** Professor and Chair of Pastoral Studies Department,
> Moody Bible Institute

"Regardless of one's theological view of law and gospel, these biblical repasts are a good chew."

> **Jim Elliff,** Christian Communicators Worldwide

"Joe Thorn has written a series of devotions that are concise and clear but also profound and penetrating. This is just the sort of resource that frazzled and frayed people (like this pastor!) need to read to come back to center and be refreshed by the wonder of the gospel and the beauty and majesty of the Lord Jesus Christ."

> **Chris Brauns,** Pastor, The Red Brick Church, Stillman Valley,
> Illinois; author, *Unpacking Forgiveness*

"*Note to Self* teaches you a skill that will permanently change your life: the skill of preaching to yourself. This is a forgotten habit in our day, and Joe Thorn winsomely models how to resurrect this lost art. *Note to Self* models what I want to see more of in my life and in the lives of the people I pastor. Practice what this book preaches and your life will be different."

> **Justin Buzzard,** Lead Pastor, Garden City Church,
> San Jose, California; blogger, *BuzzardBlog.com*

"It's not enough to simply call people to the gospel. We must help them make the connections between the gospel and their everyday living. Joe Thorn's *Note to Self* is gospel proclamation and application at its best. I will put this in the hands of my people."

> **Daniel Montgomery,** Lead Pastor, Sojourn Community Church,
> Louisville, Kentucky

NOTE
TO
SELF

NOTE
TO
SELF

THE DISCIPLINE OF
PREACHING TO YOURSELF

JOE THORN
FOREWORD BY SAM STORMS

:: CROSSWAY®

WHEATON, ILLINOIS

Note to Self: The Discipline of Preaching to Yourself

Copyright © 2011 by Joe Thorn

Published by Crossway
        1300 Crescent Street
        Wheaton, Illinois 60187

Cover design: Patrick Mahoney of The Mahoney Design Team

First printing 2011

Printed in the United States of America

Trade paperback ISBN: 978-1-4335-2206-2
PDF ISBN: 978-1-4335-2207-9
Mobipocket ISBN: 978-1-4335-2208-6
ePub ISBN: 978-1-4335-2211-6

Library of Congress Cataloging-in-Publication Data
   Thorn, Joe, 1972–
   Note to self : the discipline of preaching to yourself / Joe Thorn.
      p. cm.
   ISBN 978-1-4335-2206-2 (tpb)
   1. Meditations. 2. Christian life. II. Title.
BV4832.3.T49   2011
248.3'4—dc22   2010040122

Crossway is a publishing ministry of Good News Publishers.

VP		25	24	23	22	21	20	19
21	20	19	18	17	16	15	14	13

To my wife

Jen

who speaks words of truth and grace to me
more consistently and effectively
than anyone else.

CONTENTS

PART THREE: THE GOSPEL AND YOU

FOREWORD

One of the annoying things about forewords to books is how they so often simply repeat, in only slightly different terms, what the book itself says. That really doesn't help anyone, so I won't spend time saying in fewer words what Joe Thorn says so well in the pages that lie ahead. Let me take this opportunity, instead, to say something about why this book is worth the investment of your time and energy.

Contrary to what you may have concluded when you read the title and subtitle of this book, it is not an exercise in narcissistic introspection. This book is not an invitation to some weird form of spiritual navel-gazing as if the answers to your questions or the solutions to your problems are on the inside, somewhere in the depths of your soul. They are, in fact, on the outside. They are found not in what you do or feel for God, but in what God has graciously done for you. They are not found in your future accomplishments but in his past achievement in the life, death, and resurrection of Jesus Christ. This is, in fact, the most important "note to self" that Joe could possibly communicate.

This book is written on the heartfelt assumption that the truth of God's written Word is unparalleled in its capacity to change a human life. What ultimately accounts for the sort of transformation that we prize and that pleases God is the truth of Scripture inspired, illumined, and applied to the human soul. Good intentions, New Year's resolutions, promises, plans, personal discipline, and rigorous regimens designed to control and direct human choices only go so far. They rarely, if ever, effect a lasting and fruitful change in the soul. It is only when our thoughts are challenged and conformed to the principles of God's Word and our hearts are energized to make choices consistent with God's revealed will that a human being is transformed. Joe's book is grounded in this truth.

What I'm talking about, and what this book so beautifully portrays, is the *functional* authority of Scripture in the life of a believer. Merely affirming that the Bible is *inspired* accomplishes very little. Asserting its *authority* isn't much better. The inspiration and authority of the Scriptures are of value to us only so far as we change our beliefs to conform to its principles and alter our behavior to coincide with its imperatives. The Bible is meant to govern our lives, to fashion our choices, to challenge our cherished traditions, and ultimately to make us look more like Jesus. The question for each of us, then, is whether the Bible actually functions in this way. Do we submit to its dictates? Do we put our confidence in its promises? Do we stop living a certain way in response to its counsel? Do we embrace particular truths on its authority? Do we set aside traditional practices that conflict with its instruction? In other words, for the Bible to be of value to us it must *actually function* to shape how we think, feel, and act, as well as what we believe, value, and teach.

Reading *Note to Self* will challenge you in precisely this way. It is a no-holds-barred appeal to expose our lives to the searing searchlight of Scripture and to let its voice speak to the way we formulate our beliefs and relate to other people and think about God and make choices in the course of daily life. If you are not yet persuaded that Scripture has been invested with this sort of power, perhaps you should consider a few relevant texts before you immerse yourself in Joe's wise counsel.

Consider how this is articulated by the apostle Peter in his first epistle. He declares that we have "been born again, not of perishable seed but of imperishable, through the living and abiding word of God" (1 Pet. 1:23). This, says the apostle, is *God's* Word, not man's word, not human speculation, but the transcript of divine speech. We would be in an utterly helpless, hopeless, and spiritually pathetic condition if left to our own thoughts and agendas and wisdom. Paul applauded the Thessalonians because "when you received the word of God, which you heard from us, you accepted it not as the word of men but as what it really is, the word of God, which is at work in you believers" (1 Thess. 2:13).

This "word," says Peter, so ably interpreted and applied in Joe's book, is "imperishable" (1 Pet. 1:23). This notion of something being *imperishable* is profoundly important to Peter as he earlier declared that our heavenly inheritance is "imperishable" (that is to say, not subject to corruption or decay or defilement; 1:3–4). Again in chapter one of his epistle, Peter affirms that the ransom price by which we are set free from sin, the blood of Christ, is "imperishable" (unlike silver and gold; 1:18–19). Now here in 1 Peter 1:23 he affirms that the divine instrument by which we are born again is an "imperishable" seed, namely, the Word of God. It is imperishable as contrasted with the grass and flowers that blossom for a season but soon fade away and lose their capacity to enthrall us or satisfy us, both physically and aesthetically. The written Word and the gospel it proclaims will never die or suffer decay, notwithstanding the objections thrown at it by critics and Christ-deniers.

As if that were not enough, this "word" is "living and abiding" (1 Pet. 1:23). It is "living" because it has the power to impart life. It is abiding because the life it imparts is permanent and sustained and never dies. The contrast, of course, is not between the Word of God and literal grass and flowers. The latter are cited as representative or symbolic of anything in which we put our confidence, particularly things that are flashy and exciting and bring initial joy, but over time fade and diminish and lose their capacity to guide us and satisfy our souls, whether strength, power, wealth, beauty, or fame.

Experts study sociological dynamics and trends in order to set the agenda for how we should "do" church and organize our ministries. With all due respect to sociology, in ten years studies will show that what used to work is now passé and ineffective. *And through it all the Word of God will have remained true and unchanging and ever powerful.*

Others study psychological factors that supposedly govern human behavior and provide us with sure-fire formulas for better living and emotional and mental health. With all due respect to psychology, in ten years new studies and additional research will overturn and veto what was earlier believed to be true, perhaps even offering advice entirely opposite to what we were given years before. *And through it all the Word of God will have remained true and unchanging and ever powerful.*

The learned study philosophy and political theory and economic trends and church growth models and community dynamics and principles that govern interpersonal relationships. And with all due respect to the brilliance of such people and the short-term help they bring us, in ten years the pendulum will have swung back, and we will be told to ignore earlier discoveries and to embrace yet another theory of what makes life work and what enhances the testimony of the church and what will serve to improve our physical and spiritual welfare. *And through it all the Word of God will have remained true and unchanging and ever powerful.*

The price of gold may rise and fall. The stock market may prove bullish or bearish. Your physical appearance will improve and then disintegrate. The loyalty of friends will come and go. Earthly fame will last but for a season. *And through it all, the truths and principles and life-giving power of God's Word will remain.*

Let it be the anchor for your soul. Let it be the rock on which you stand. Let it be the compass to guide you through trials and tragic times. Let it govern your choices and renew your heart and restore your joy and ground your hope. Build your life on its moral principles. Embrace its ethical and moral norms. Believe what it says about the nature of God. Believe what it says about the nature of mankind.

Peter isn't finished, and neither am I. This glorious, imperishable, living, and abiding Word of God is itself the *catalyst and cause of spiritual growth and maturity*. It is by or through the pure spiritual milk of the Word that "you may grow up into salvation" (1 Pet. 2:2). Peter is not saying here that the Christians to whom he is writing were newly converted or that they were immature. He says they are "like" newborn infants insofar as they should crave life-sustaining spiritual milk even as a baby craves life-sustaining physical milk from his/her mother. We are all "infants" or babies insofar as we've all been begotten or born of the sovereign grace of our heavenly Father. And it is "by it," that is, by means of the pure spiritual milk of the Word that we grow up into salvation, that we mature and deepen in our faith, that we come to trust God more and more each day, that we find the strength to resist temptation, the passion to serve the poor, and the boldness to reach out to those who have no hope.

Through the power of the Holy Spirit, God has invested the biblical text with the capacity to change human lives and transform the experience of the church. Other texts are equally emphatic in making this point. The Word of God is the spring from which the waters of *faith* arise, for Paul says in Romans 10:17 that "faith comes from hearing" and that hearing comes "by the word of Christ." It is from or through the Scriptures that the Spirit imparts *perseverance and encouragement*. This is Paul's point in Romans 15:4, "For whatever was written in earlier times was written for our instruction, that through perseverance and the encouragement of the Scriptures we might have hope" (NASB). In a similar vein,

Paul declares that it is from or through the Scriptures that *joy and peace* arise. He prays in Romans 15:13 that God would "fill you with all joy and peace in believing, so that by the power of the Holy Spirit you may abound in hope." It is only "as" you believe or "because" you believe or "in connection with" believing that these affections become yours. The point is that God most assuredly will *not* fill you abundantly with these affections if you *don't* believe. Both joy and peace are therefore the fruit of *believing*, which in turn yields hope.

The Word of God also accounts for the ongoing operation of the *miraculous* in the body of Christ. We read in Galatians 3:5, "Does He who provides you with the Spirit and works miracles among you, do it by the works of the Law, or by hearing with faith?" (NASB). The instrument God uses to bring miracles into our midst is the faith that we experience *upon hearing the Word of God!* When we hear the Word of God (in preaching and teaching and private study and reading books such as *Note to Self*), our thoughts and hearts become God centered; our focus is on his glory and thus our faith in his greatness expands and our confidence in his ability to work miracles deepens, all of which is the soil in which the seeds of the supernatural are sown.

It is the Word of God, expounded and explained and applied (which Joe does so beautifully in this short volume), that yields the fruit of sanctification and holiness in daily life. A few passages make this abundantly clear. In 1 Thessalonians 2:13 we read, "And we also thank God constantly for this, that when you received the word of God, which you heard from us, you accepted it not as the word of men but as what it really is, the word of God, *which is at work in you believers.*" Again, "In pointing out these things to the brethren, you will be a good servant of Christ Jesus, *constantly nourished on the words of the faith and of the sound doctrine* which you have been following" (1 Tim. 4:6 NASB). Finally, the Word of God "is living and active and sharper than any two-edged sword, and piercing as far as the division of soul and spirit, both of joints and marrow, and able to judge the thoughts and intentions of the heart" (Heb. 4:12 NASB).

This Word of God is to be *earnestly desired* and *sought after* and *longed for* (1 Pet. 2:2). When I hear Peter exhort us to "long for" the Word I am reminded of Psalm 119 and I'm rebuked by the passion of the psalmist:

> "In the way of your testimonies *I delight as much as in all riches*" (v. 14).
>
> "*My soul is consumed with longing* for your rules at all times" (v. 20).
>
> "Behold, *I long* for your precepts" (v. 40).
>
> "For I find my *delight* in your commandments, *which I love*" (v. 47).
>
> "The law of your mouth is *better to me than thousands of gold and silver pieces*" (v. 72).
>
> "*Oh how I love your law!*" (v. 97).
>
> "How *sweet* are your words to my taste, *sweeter than honey to my mouth*!" (v. 103).
>
> "Your testimonies are my heritage forever, for they are *the joy of my heart*" (v. 111).
>
> "Therefore *I love your commandments above gold, above fine gold*" (v. 127).

"I *rejoice* at your word like one who finds great spoil" (v. 162).

"My soul keeps your testimonies; *I love them exceedingly*" (v. 167).

Peter's point, my point, and Joe's point, is simply this: crave the Word of God. Be desperate for it! Seek it. Yearn for it. Long for it. Desire it. Tolerate nothing in your life that might diminish your hunger for God's Word. And apply it with vigor and spiritual energy!

The Word of God, whether it is preached and heard or read and memorized, is more than simply true. It is effectual. The Word of God does more than merely announce: it accomplishes! It doesn't just impart information: it creates life! Someone once said, and rightly so, that God speaking is God acting. God's Word is always carried along by God's Spirit and empowered to produce what it proclaims.

This, then, is the rationale for Joe's book. And this is why it is so deserving of your careful and attentive reading.

Sam Storms
Senior Pastor
Bridgeway Church
Oklahoma City, OK

ACKNOWLEDGMENTS

I would like to thank Justin Taylor for originally encouraging me to write this book and Mattie Wolf for her help as my editor.

Thanks to Steve McCoy, who has been a constant encouragement for me over the years to stay focused on Jesus, my family, and the church (in that order).

Thanks to the leadership and congregation of Redeemer Fellowship of St. Charles, Illinois, who are a wonderful church family, exemplifying unity around Christ's gospel and mission, and to the members of the Acts 29 Network, who both call for and also model the discipline of preaching the gospel to others and themselves.

INTRODUCTION
PREACHING TO OURSELVES?

Christians value the preaching of Scripture and are genuinely excited when it is preached well (when God and the gospel are on full display). We like being challenged by the Word, and we need the comfort that comes from the heralding of God's promises to all who believe. We need good preaching. Yet many who value the preaching of Scripture by pastors and teachers are not benefiting from the kind of preaching that should be most consistent and personal—preaching to ourselves.

The idea of preaching the gospel to ourselves is getting more press these days, but the actual work of preaching to ourselves seems to be slow in coming. We hear the basic concept and think, "Of course, I need to do that." But where do we start? What does it mean? How do we actually do it?

Let me begin by saying I think we need to talk a bit more broadly about this kind of private preaching. It is not just gospel that we need to preach to ourselves, but law and gospel. Just as the lost cannot come to know Christ apart from an understanding of law and gospel, neither will the believer grow in grace apart from the preaching of both law and gospel. I am hopeful that this brief introduction to the idea of preaching to ourselves will prove to be a helpful clarification and practical explanation of this spiritual discipline.

Let's start with a definition. Preaching to ourselves is the personal act of applying the law and the gospel to our own lives with the aim of experiencing the transforming grace of God leading to ongoing faith, repentance, and greater godliness. It is critically important to sit under the preaching of the Word in your local church. Additionally, we can listen to podcasts and read books as God continues to work through his Word to impact our lives. But even in the midst of all of this listening, it is not enough to hear; we must take the Word preached and continue to preach it to ourselves.

Good preaching always shows how truth is relevant, applicable, or experiential, but preachers can only take the Word so far. They do not know what lies in our hearts or the specific ways in which we may be struggling with doubt, fear, or failure. When hearing the Word preached, we still must apply it to our own hearts and lives. Therefore, my explanation of preaching to ourselves is applicable to those times when we hear another preach the Word to us, as well as when we take in God's Word privately.

This personal, devotional work is essential to our own health, but also to our effectiveness in sharing the law and the gospel with others. The more deeply we understand and experience law and gospel, the more capable we become in communicating and applying it to those around us. A good teacher or evangelist is first a good preacher to himself.

PREACHING THE LAW TO OURSELVES

This renewed interest in preaching the gospel to ourselves is good, but the gospel will remain cloudy, if not irrelevant, to us if we do not understand the law of God. When the Bible talks about God's law, it can take on different meanings depending on the author and the context. The law can be understood as the commands of God, the Scripture as a whole, or even a mistaken approach to God's commands that leads people away from the gospel. For our purposes we are considering the law of God as his revealed will and standard of righteousness. This is summarized as loving God and neighbor, is organized in the Decalogue, and is taught in detail by the prophets, the apostles, and Jesus himself.

As we look at the law with the aim of preaching it well, we need to understand its purpose. Essentially, the law shows us three things: it shows us what's right, what's wrong, and what's needed.

The Law Shows Us What's Right

The commands of God reveal his will to us and serve as a rule for godly living. This is in itself, grace. It means that God has not left us alone in ignorance concerning what is truly right or wrong. While the law of God is something we intuitively, if partially, know because we are made in his image, in our sinful condition we repress that knowledge and fight against our consciences when they alert us to our own wrongdoing. We need his law more than we need a vague admonition to "love" and "worship."

Thankfully God's law is not a collection of cloudy exhortations. He has not left us with unclear generalities about loving God and neighbor, but he has told us what he wants from us with great specificity. God commands us to care for the poor, the fatherless, and the widow. He calls his people to give generously, and to be kind and hospitable to the sojourner among them. He tells husbands how to love their wives, wives how to honor their husbands, children how to honor their parents, and parents how to raise their children. God's law tells us what sin is, and that we must reject it and pursue the righteousness reflected in his commands. The law shows us what is right.

This is grace, that God has given us his clear and understandable Word. And yet, the clarity of the law becomes a problem for us, as sinners, for we know as soon as we start that we cannot keep this law. The law not only shows us what's right but also what's wrong.

The Law Shows Us What's Wrong

So in one sense, the law functions like a window opening up the truth of God's will for us, but, it also works like a mirror reflecting our own failure and corruption back to us. The plain truth is, we do not, and cannot, keep God's law. As the apostle Paul writes in Romans 7:7, "If it had not been for the law, I would not have known sin. For I would not have known what it is to covet if the law had not said, 'You shall not covet.'"

The law, in showing us what is right, immediately shows us what is wrong—we are lawbreakers. This is its second purpose, to expose our sin and unbelief and make known our condemnation. But the law's work is not done in showing us our own failure. By showing us what's wrong, it also shows us what's desperately needed.

The Law Shows Us What's Needed

In exposing our own corruption, the law of God leaves us guilty and points us to our need for redemption. We are lawbreakers and need forgiveness, cleansing, and restoration. In this sense the law serves as a guide in leading us to the gospel. It fits us for it, prepares us for it. The law, while being "holy and righteous and good," is itself not good news. It is the bad news that makes the good news of the gospel so relevant. In this way, the law prepares us for the gospel by showing us our need for it.

In preaching the law to ourselves we see and admire God's will and way, while exposing and confessing our sinfulness. This leads us toward the gospel where we find our only hope of redemption and restoration. Preaching the law to ourselves breaks our pride, leads to humility, and calls us to cry out to God and depend on his mercy.

One of the primary ways we can do this is by asking a lot of questions, not just of the text, but of ourselves.

- What does God require of me?
- Since God wants more than superficial, external obedience, what internal qualities are required to keep this law well?
- How do I keep this law externally but not internally?
- How do I feel about this command?

Paul's words in Romans 7:7–25 give a good example of one who knows how to preach to himself. Notice how Paul is speaking of himself in such a personal way that it is clear that what he shares with the church in Rome is something he has preached to himself.

What then shall we say? That the law is sin? By no means! Yet if it had not been for the law, I would not have known sin. For I would not have known what it is to covet if the law had not said, "You shall not covet." But sin, seizing an opportunity through the commandment, produced in me all kinds of covetousness. For apart from the law, sin lies dead. I was once alive apart from the law, but when the commandment came, sin came alive and I died. The very commandment that promised life proved to be death to me. For sin, seizing an opportunity through the commandment, deceived me and through it killed me. So the law is holy, and the commandment is holy and righteous and good.

Did that which is good, then, bring death to me? By no means! It was sin, producing death in me through what is good, in order that sin might be shown to be sin, and through the commandment might become sinful beyond measure. For we know that the law is spiritual, but I am of the flesh, sold under sin. For I do not understand my own actions. For I do not do what I want, but I do the very thing I hate. Now if I do what I do not want, I agree with the law, that it is good. So now it is no longer I who do it, but sin that dwells within me. For I know that nothing good dwells in me, that is, in my flesh. For I have the desire to do what is right, but not the ability to carry it out. For I do not do the good I want, but the evil I do not want is what I keep on doing. Now if I do what I do not want, it is no longer I who do it, but sin that dwells within me.

So I find it to be a law that when I want to do right, evil lies close at hand. For I delight in the law of God, in my inner being, but I see in my members another law waging war against the law of my mind and making me captive to the law of sin that dwells in my members. Wretched man that I am! Who will deliver me from this body of death? Thanks be to God through Jesus Christ our Lord! So then, I myself serve the law of God with my mind, but with my flesh I serve the law of sin.

Here we can see how Paul interacts with the law in a very personal way that leads him through the marvel at God's law (that which is good), conviction over his own lawlessness (that which is wrong), and his hunger for redemption (that which is needed).

- What's right: "So the law is holy, and the commandment is holy and righteous and good."
- What's wrong: "For I know that nothing good dwells in me, that is, in my flesh. For I have the desire to do what is right, but not the ability to carry it out."
- What's needed: "Wretched man that I am! Who will deliver me from this body of death?"

In preaching the law to himself, Paul led himself back to his only hope, the gospel.

PREACHING THE GOSPEL TO OURSELVES

We cannot properly preach the law without also preaching the gospel, for God has not given us his law as the end. But before we consider how to preach the gospel, it will be helpful to clarify the gospel itself. In one sense we must say that the gospel is history. It happened. Simply put, the gospel is the life, death, and resurrection of Jesus. Yet these events have meaning that needs to be explained. In the Bible, "gospel" is not something we do but something we believe. It is the good news of what Jesus accomplished in his life, death, and resurrection.

At its core, the gospel is Jesus as the substitute for sinners. We could summarize the whole by saying that in his life Jesus lives in perfect submission to the will of God and he fulfills his righteous standard (the law). In his death on the cross he quenches God's wrath against sin, satisfying the sovereign demand for justice. In his resurrection he is victorious over sin and death. All of this is done on behalf of sinners in need of redemption and is offered to all who believe. This is therefore very "good news."

Jesus' life is good news, for his obedience to the Father and fulfillment of the law is for us. Where we as sinners fail to keep the law, Jesus was perfectly faithful. Jesus' death is good news because his death was a payment for our sin, and by it we are cleansed from our guilt and released from condemnation. Jesus' resurrection is good news because his victory over death is ours and through it we look forward to a resurrection of our own.

When we get to the business of preaching this good news to ourselves, we are essentially denying self and resting in the grace of Christ in his life, death, and resurrection. But this means we have to know how the gospel addresses our current spiritual state, whether happy, sad, afraid, broken, proud, weak, or self-righteous.

Jesus Is Your Righteousness (His Life)

The life of Jesus offers hope to the broken, to those who recognize their inability to keep God's law, and to those who are frustrated with their falling and failings. The gospel is the life of Jesus for sinners. His righteousness is our righteousness, and this gives us hope and confidence before God. Here the broken find encouragement, for in Christ we are righteous.

Jesus Is Your Forgiveness (His Death)

The death of Jesus offers hope to those who are overcome with guilt and conviction by offering cleansing and acceptance. Though we are sinners, God will not count our sins against us. He receives us because Jesus has died and put away our sins and reconciled us to God, who now, and forever, relates to us as a father relates to his son, and nothing can separate us from his love. Here the broken find hope, for in Christ we are cleansed.

Jesus Is Your Victory (His Resurrection)

The resurrection of Jesus offers courage and strength to persevere because his victory over sin and death is ours both in this life and in the one to come. The same spirit that raised Jesus from the dead dwells in us, sanctifies us, and empowers us to follow Christ and serve the mission of the church. And we know that the spirit who raised Jesus from the dead will raise us as well when Jesus returns. Here the broken find hope and courage, for in Christ we have power and victory to obey, and we will, in the end, be raised in his likeness.

PREACHING LAW AND GOSPEL TOGETHER

Neither the law nor the gospel can stand on its own in our preaching. The law is given to show us God's way and our brokenness, so that we will see our need for redemption. In the gospel we find our redemption, but we are then eager to look afresh at the law. Now we see it as a delight to carry out, because even though we cannot keep the law perfectly, Jesus has kept it perfectly for us. Our imperfect obedience brings pleasure to God because of Christ's substitution. Therefore preaching to ourselves puts us into a cycle of law and gospel where we move from our guilt and need to God's grace and provision and then back to the law as joyful and free obedience.

The impact of preaching to ourselves is not found in dramatic moments of crisis, or in our ability to use words creatively, but in the ongoing, regular, and virtually plain preaching of the law and the gospel. Preaching to ourselves is, in a practical sense, like reading notes you have written to yourself. They will often amount to important reminders about who we really are in ourselves and in Christ.

Preaching to yourself demands asking a lot of questions, both of God's Word and especially of yourself. You will have to ask and be honest about your motives, struggles, and needs. You will need to clarify to yourself what God's law means in principle, but also what it requires specifically of you. You will need to ask how the gospel meets your needs and heals your brokenness. To preach to yourself is to challenge yourself, push yourself, and point yourself to the truth. It is not so much uncovering new truth as much as it is reminding yourself of the truth you tend to forget.

PART ONE
THE GOSPEL AND GOD

1
LOVE

For this is the message that you have heard from the beginning,
that we should love one another.
We should not be like Cain, who was of the evil one and
murdered his brother.
And why did he murder him? Because his own deeds were evil and
his brother's righteous.
Do not be surprised, brothers, that the world hates you.
We know that we have passed out of death into life, because we love
the brothers. Whoever does not love abides in death.
Everyone who hates his brother is a murderer, and you know that no
murderer has eternal life abiding in him.
By this we know love, that he laid down his life for us, and we ought
to lay down our lives for the brothers.
But if anyone has the world's goods and sees his brother in need,
yet closes his heart against him, how does God's love abide in him?
Little children, let us not love in word or talk but
in deed and in truth.

1 JOHN 3:11–18

Dear Self,

You have found that the command to love can be both inspiring and suffocating. On the one hand, you are made to love and want to love like Jesus. On the other hand, you know your own weaknesses, and the people God calls you to love aren't always the most lovable. But as with all of the commands of

God, you must not only see what God asks of you but also how he has met that need himself in the gospel on your behalf. This is especially true in the case of love.

You must love God and your neighbor, but only one can give birth to the other. Do you recall that the command to love God with all one's heart, mind, soul, and strength was the command that drove Martin Luther to hate God? It was a command that he could not meet, and the righteous standard of God nearly drove him mad. You are like Luther. Love is something beyond your ability as well, yet the command remains.

The reality is that you only love God because he loved you first. He loved you before you were born and chose you for himself. His love for you secured your salvation, and because you have experienced his life-redeeming love you love him in return.

But for love to continue and grow, and for you to love the unlovable, it is important that you meditate on the gospel. Get this—you only know what love really is by looking to your Savior. And we learn it from him continually, not just once. You must daily go to the cross and see your Savior's love for the unlovable (that means you).

You must learn, relearn, and remember your Savior's love and sacrifice for the wicked, the rebellious, the black-hearted—for people like you. And when you see the Holy One's sacrificial love for you, you not only see what love looks like, but also you find strength and power to love like him.

2
REJOICE

Make a joyful noise to the LORD, all the earth!
Serve the LORD with gladness!
Come into his presence with singing!
Know that the LORD, he is God!
It is he who made us, and we are his;
we are his people, and the sheep of his pasture.
Enter his gates with thanksgiving,
and his courts with praise!
Give thanks to him; bless his name!
For the LORD is good;
his steadfast love endures forever,
and his faithfulness to all generations.

PSALM 100

Dear Self,

I know, you see those words and you often ponder them with both longing and frustration. Joy? The way the psalmist describes it often leaves you with the impression that this kind of happiness is not real, but just an amplified expression of what you experience in small, real-life measure. Or you think that it is just a short burst of emotion that arises in a moment of deep worship. But let's be honest, the reason you do not experience the joy you read about in Scripture is because your heart is divided, and your interests are spread thin.

Why the call for joy? Why can all of creation sing and serve its Creator with gladness? Because he really is God. "Know that the LORD, he is God!" At times you have found yourself wondering, "Is this real? God, the Bible, Jesus, Satan, sin, and salvation—is it all real?" You don't admit that to those around you, but there are times when you question it all. And in his grace God confirms by his Word and Spirit that it is true. He is God! And the reality of your theology gives you joy.

What you believe is not a religious game, or a manmade crutch upon which you lean for a little assistance. Rather it is the divinely revealed truth that makes you who you are and gives you cause to rejoice. You can rejoice not only because he is God, but because we are his people, and as such he protects us and provides for us in all ways necessary for us to know him more fully, enjoy him more deeply, and make him known more widely.

And you can rejoice because his love remains over you now and always. It never dries up, runs low, or fades out. His love endures forever. Because of all this, and so much more, you can know the joy the psalmists describe in their songs. You just need to return to these truths. You need reminding.

3

FEAR

The fear of the LORD is the beginning of wisdom;
all those who practice it have a good understanding.
His praise endures forever!

PSALM 111:10

And do not fear those who kill the body but cannot kill the soul.
Rather fear him who can destroy both soul and body in hell.

MATTHEW 10:28

Dear Self,

You often fear the wrong things. For example, often you are fearful of conflict, suffering, or the loss of good things like respect or acceptance by certain kinds of people. It is understandable from a worldly perspective, for these things you are afraid of losing are themselves—worldly. This does not mean they are bad, but they are temporal. So many of the things you value are good gifts from God; but they do not last, nor are they supposed to be something from which you find your identity and lasting hope.

The problem with this kind of worldly fear is that it will lead you to toe party lines instead of correcting and challenging the people you are close to. It will compel you to try to live a safe life, free from risk or danger instead of being willing to make the hard and "risky" choice of following Jesus in a culture that rejects him. It will lead you to so prize the good gifts of God that they mutate into idols that you are unwilling to let go of.

You don't need to be afraid of anything, but you do need to fear your God with a holy reverence. Such "fear" is an aspect of faith that responds to God's holiness, sovereignty, and transcendence. This higher form of fear is that which leads to awe, adoration, and carefulness of life because of the intimate knowledge of your Maker and Redeemer. What should you fear in life above a holy God who forgives the sins of unholy men like yourself? What can be taken from you? Your possessions can go up in flames, but you have treasure in heaven and stand to inherit the kingdom. Your reputation may be sullied, but you are justified in Jesus. You may be rejected by those you admire, but you are accepted by God. You may be hated, but your Father in heaven loves you with an undying love. What is there in this life to fear?

The fear you need to maintain and cultivate is a fear of God, for in it you will discover wisdom and develop strength that enables you to persevere in faith to the end.

4

SING

Sing praises to the LORD, O you his saints,
and give thanks to his holy name.

PSALM 30:4

Dear Self,

You really should sing more. You should sing more than at gathered worship with the church. You should sing in the car, while working in the yard, and in your home. And when you sing, you should do so with more than lungs and lips. You should sing with your heart, mind, and soul.

And stop rolling your eyes! I'm not suggesting that you become the perpetually happy whistler who rolls through the aisles of the grocery store whistling others into an incurable state of annoyance. But song does need to be a much bigger part of your life.

People sing about the things that capture their hearts and things that give them joy. People sing of heroes, victory, longing, and hope. People even sing as a way to express their sorrow. Does anyone have more reasons to sing than you? As a sinner who has been forgiven, a slave who has been freed, a blind man who has received sight, a spiritual cripple who has been healed—all by the gospel—you have real reasons to be known as a person of song!

It is one thing to tell the world of God's work of redemption in Jesus; it is another to sing of it. Anyone can parrot truth, but to sing of it—from the soul—reveals how you feel. Song is the natural and appropriate response to the gospel, because singing is one of the highest expressions of joy.

So why aren't you singing "always, only for [your] king?"[1] Have the mercies of God grown small in your heart? Is there little joy, little gratitude, little wonder? Do you just not feel like singing? The confession of your sins and gospel meditation will lead you to song, so start there. There are songs of praise, thanksgiving, confession, lament, and victory that need your voice.

From the great hymns of old to the new songs echoing the wonders of God's mercy, you have more means of finding songs of redemption than any other generation before you. So join the chorus of God's people, who have always been known as a people who sing.

---

[1] Frances R. Havergal, "Take My Life and Let It Be," 1874.

5

GIVE THANKS

Enter his gates with thanksgiving,
and his courts with praise!
Give thanks to him; bless his name!
For the LORD is good;
his steadfast love endures forever,
and his faithfulness to all generations.

PSALM 100:4–5

Dear Self,

When was the last time you used the word "thanksgiving" without referencing to the holiday? Yes, it is appropriate that you "give thanks" at the dinner table, but this easily becomes a formality void of real affection. Thankfulness is the joyful and humble response of a heart that has been transformed by grace.

The psalmist calls us to "enter his gates with thanksgiving and praise," which is a call to approach God in gratitude. Why is that? He points to three realities: because God is good, because God is loving, and because God is faithful. A good theologian is thankful, and until you know these truths you are likely to feel entitled and deserving.

How do you know God to be good, loving, and faithful? These attributes were put on display most beautifully in the gospel. God is good, loving, and faithful by not giving you what you deserve (judgment) and by lavishing on you grace unmeasured. He is good and loving in saving us from sin and judgment, giving us hope and life, and adopting us as his own. He is faithful to his Word and his promise to us, that he will not count our sins against us and will continue the work he began in us to completion. On top of this, every good thing you have in this life is a gift from your heavenly Father, and as one who has been justified by the grace of Christ you should see everything in your life as grace that accompanies your salvation. For such things do not come from a Judge, but your Dad.

Does gratitude characterize your thoughts of God? Thankfulness is a good test of your faith. Its absence demonstrates that your faith is more lip service than experiential knowledge. Your days, whether easy or difficult, should be filled with thanksgiving because while life changes drastically, your God remains the same forever. He is constant—constantly good, loving, and faithful.

6

REMEMBER YOUR SINS

I acknowledged my sin to you,
and I did not cover my iniquity;
I said, "I will confess my transgressions to the LORD,"
and you forgave the iniquity of my sin.

PSALM 32:5

Dear Self,

Yes, part of your confidence before God is that he has forgiven you of your sins and remembers them no more. But sometimes you have a hard time forgetting all that you have done wrong. Of course, God doesn't actually forget your sins. He remains omniscient, knowing everything all the time. Saying God does not remember your sins is a way of saying he will not hold them against you as judge. He has thoroughly forgiven you in Jesus. You need to hear that. Those who believe in Jesus are truly forgiven. Yet, recalling your sins can lead to a perverted relationship between guilt and pride, which is a very popular method for dealing with the feeling of guilt. It works like this.

You are aware of the sins you have committed and consequently feel guilt—paralyzing guilt that says you are unworthy of even talking to God. Seriously, some of the things you have done are pretty messed up. As you consider your sins and feel their weight, you decide to embrace the guilt and even heap it on. Then, only after you have felt sufficiently bad about all that you have been and done do you begin to feel better about it all. It's as if amassing feelings of guilt becomes a perverted kind of penance in which you pay for your transgression by making yourself feel bad—as if your guilt is a means of getting clean. It may be hard to see it, but you can probably remember times when you felt as if you could not approach God because of your sin. So you waited, heaped on the guilt, and after you felt bad enough and sorry enough, you began to try to draw near to God as if you had somehow become more acceptable.

Look, the memory of your sins is no cause to beat yourself up and wallow in guilt. Instead, it should lead you to rejoice in the redemption you have in Jesus. So you will (and should) remember your sins but not be plagued by them. As a Christian you must see them in light of the cross. You need to remember your sins for what they are—lawlessness that stemmed from a heart that hated God. It wasn't just what you did; it was what you were. And in remembering these sins, you hold fast to Jesus. This remembrance does not encourage you to shrink back from God but to draw near, seeking him because of the hope of the gospel. When you remember your sins, you learn humility, love Jesus, and make much of the gospel.

7

JESUS IS BIG

And being found in human form, he humbled himself by becoming
obedient to the point of death, even death on a cross.
Therefore God has highly exalted him and bestowed on him the name
that is above every name,
so that at the name of Jesus every knee should bow,
in heaven and on earth and under the earth,
and every tongue confess that Jesus Christ is Lord,
to the glory of God the Father.

PHILIPPIANS 2:8–11

Dear Self,

Take note—your view of Jesus tends to shrink over time. It is not that your theology itself drifts, but sometimes you so focus on one aspect of Jesus that you tend to forget the rest. The result is a shrinking Jesus (in your faith). And as your shrinking Jesus becomes small Jesus, he is easily eclipsed by your idols and ego.

The bigger and more biblical your understanding of who Jesus is, the more likely he is to be such an object of love and adoration that the idols that aim at capturing your attention and swaying your allegiance will lose their power. This is why you sometimes lack earnestness for the kingdom and the glory of God while you overflow with passion concerning temporal things. Instead of making a joyful noise and singing earnestly for the victory Christ has over sin and death, you express a dispassionate approval and mouth the words to the songs sung in worship. But there is often fire in your belly and shouts of joy when your favorite college football team is victorious over the competition. This is probably why the church is shrinking in North America—because small Jesus does not inspire awe, command respect, lead to worship, or compel us to talk of him (much less suffer for him). And small Jesus is too little to arrest the attention of the world.

So please remember—Jesus is bigger than you tend to think. He is the perfect revelation of God, the radiance of his glory, the exact imprint of his nature; he is the Creator and Sustainer of all that exists. Everything belongs to him and exists for him. He is the author of your salvation, the perfecter of your faith, and the only one in whom you can find life.

8

JESUS IS ENOUGH

I have learned in whatever situation I am to be content.
I know how to be brought low, and I know how to abound.
In any and every circumstance, I have learned the secret of
facing plenty and hunger,
abundance and need.
I can do all things through him who strengthens me.

PHILIPPIANS 4:11–13

Dear Self,

Are you satisfied? It is pretty obvious that the answer is often no. I am not saying it is wrong to want things in this life, but why do you find yourself so frustrated with the absence of those things? The problem is not that you want evil things. The things you want are generally good, or at least harmless in themselves. But more than wanting, you become frustrated by not having. You become jealous, envious, and discontented with your life. It is true; you need what you lack, but what you lack is satisfaction in Jesus.

When you find your deepest satisfaction in Jesus, you are protected from bitterness in times of want and pride in times of abundance. The world and all good gifts within it are temporal blessings. For you, Christian, their presence should remind you of the Giver, and their absence should remind you of that which never fades nor can be taken away.

Paul models this well for you. He knows the secret of being content whether he has abundance or nothing at all, for he has found his ultimate satisfaction in Jesus. On the one hand, you know what it is like to have an abundance and then struggle with the extremes of guilt and greed. Both of these responses stem from your focus on the worldly gifts themselves instead of on the generosity of the Giver of such gifts. False guilt rises up in times of abundance as you focus on your unworthiness. But this guilt only leads you deeper into an unhealthy kind of spiritual navel-gazing that ignores the goodness and generosity of God. He gives lavishly in many ways—in this life and the life to come—and all forms of his goodness to you are grounded in your union with Jesus. Greed rises up in times of abundance as you develop a sense of entitlement.

Both guilt and greed in times of abundance are the responses of your heart when Jesus is not more glorious to you than the worldly gifts God has also given. If Jesus is your greatest treasure, you respond to God's generosity in all areas of life with great joy and the desire to share what God has given you—both the worldly goods and the heavenly gospel.

On the other hand, you know what it is like to have little in this world and then struggle with jealousy and bitterness. But the root of the problem is the same—Jesus is not your greatest treasure. Jesus is enough. Do you believe that? Can you say, with the author of Hebrews, that you can be content with whatever you have because God said, "I will never leave you nor forsake you" (Heb. 13:5)? This is a promise made to us in Jesus. Jesus is enough, but that kind of satisfaction is only experienced when we understand our greatest needs to be redemption and restoration. God in Christ has reconciled us to himself, is renewing our minds, and promises to raise us from the dead, and we will dwell in righteousness and peace forever. If you have this, what more do you need?

9

GOD DOES NOT ANSWER TO YOU

Truly God is good to Israel,
to those who are pure in heart.
But as for me, my feet had almost stumbled,
my steps had nearly slipped.
For I was envious of the arrogant
when I saw the prosperity of the wicked . . .
until I went into the sanctuary of God;
then I discerned their end.

PSALM 73:1–3, 17

Dear Self,

Theology is a way for you to know and respond to God. It is something you tether to God, not something you tether God to. This is important to keep in mind when you are working out theology in your present circumstances. Even when God has clearly revealed himself, and you feel as though you have the answers to some of the big questions of life, it does not mean that your experience will always mirror what you think are the logical outworkings of those doctrines.

You know that God is sovereign and good, and that should be enough to comfort and direct you. It should calm and quiet you. It should stop your complaining and start your worship even in the midst of the most painful experiences of life. But you cannot live in that sweet spot of theology if you are using theology to tie God down in his operations.

The problem will not be with God being "consistent," but with the outworking of your own theology and what you expect from God in the most practical ways. Do not attempt to base your interpretation of God on your circumstances, but see your circumstances in light of who God has revealed himself to be. Seasons of affliction and unanswered prayer do not mean God likes to hurt you or leave you in the dark. In fact, you know the opposite is true; God works for your holiness and happiness in his Son through affliction; and even in the darkest times of life when he seems silent, he is with you to guide and protect you.

What this means for you is to remember that God does not answer to you or to your theology. You answer to him and can rest on what he has revealed of himself in his Word.

10

BE HUMBLE IN YOUR THEOLOGY

Clothe yourselves, all of you, with humility toward one another,
for "God opposes the proud but gives grace to the humble."

1 PETER 5:5

Dear Self,

A good theologian is humble. You may be known as a theologian, or at least want to be known as one, but are you also known as being humble? These two things should be inseparable.

The more robust, the more detailed your theology, the more humble you should become. Why? Because you did not figure God out; he revealed himself to you. Don't you remember the words of Jesus to Peter when the disciple correctly acknowledged Jesus as the Messiah? "Blessed are you, Simon Bar-Jonah! For flesh and blood has not revealed this to you, but my Father who is in heaven." (Matt. 16:17) The theologian owes his knowledge to God himself, who has not only made himself known in creation and Scripture but has also opened our eyes to understand and embrace the truth.

The proud theologian has somehow convinced himself, or at least acts as if, he discovered God. But you understand that you did not uncover the truth of God like some kind of rock star archeologist. He sought you, caught you, and gave you sight, knowledge, and life. Humility should be borne out of your theology because you are so entirely dependent on God for it.

You must also remember that your theology is not your own. Rather you are following in the steps of generations before you who have worked hard at knowing and making known the one true God. If you are a good theologian, part of that is because good theologians have gone before you and made a path for you to walk.

It's possible to be technically accurate in your theology and yet miss the mark of humility. Be passionate for God, fight for truth, contend for the faith, but be humble. Your knowledge is a cause to be humble, not a reason to boast in your insight or tradition.

11
ENDURE

May you be strengthened with all power,
according to his glorious might,
for all endurance and patience with joy,
giving thanks to the Father, who has qualified you
to share in the inheritance of the saints in light.
He has delivered us from the domain of darkness and
transferred us to the kingdom of his beloved Son,
in whom we have redemption, the forgiveness of sins.

COLOSSIANS 1:11–14

Dear Self,

You will never make it to the end by trying harder but by trusting more. I know this works against your natural tendency to want to take care of a situation on your own. You prefer putting your head down, getting to work, and making things happen. But this is a dangerous approach to following Christ that is sure to lead to a great fall, for faith and perseverance are not simply matters of willpower and determination. Yes, God calls you to be resolute, but in all that you are called to be and do, you will fail if you are not depending on God for the strength necessary to make it to the end.

You can endure, but not because you have put in long hours training yourself to persevere. You can endure because your God is a "God of endurance" (Rom. 15:5) who is faithful to carry out the good work he has begun in you (Phil. 1:6). You can persevere to the end because God has delivered you from the domain of darkness and has given you citizenship in the kingdom of his Son. Your new King and community stand with you so that you are not alone. To trust God more requires that you recognize your dependence, know his power and purpose, and continue by faith.

12
SEEK GOD

How can a young man keep his way pure?
By guarding it according to your word.
With my whole heart I seek you;
let me not wander from your commandments!
PSALM 119:9–10

Dear Self,

You tend to forget that seeking God is not only a quest for the lost, but is also to characterize the life of the found. The whole of your life should be seen as a seeking for God. This is not, of course, seeking for that which you do not know or have. God has found you, bought you, and owns you. You have been adopted, and nothing can separate you from the love of God in Jesus. Yet your need to seek God never ends.

Seeking God means that you are continually aiming and working at knowing him more deeply, depending on him more thoroughly, and experiencing his grace more richly. The psalmist says that his desire is to remain "pure." He wants to live uprightly and to honor God. He knows that this means he must guard his life according to God's Word, but he also recognizes that this is not just an act of willpower. It is the hope of God's sustaining grace that he finds as he seeks God.

It is unfortunate that you forget your need to seek God, for though you are right that God is enough, you forget that he is only found to be enough by those who seek him. Seeking God means that in all you do, you keep his honor in your mind, his Word in your heart, and his glory as your goal—so you are seeking to actually know him and make him known.

13

WAIT FOR JESUS

Therefore, preparing your minds for action, and being sober-minded,
set your hope fully on the grace that will be brought to you
at the revelation of Jesus Christ.

1 PETER 1:13

Dear Self,

What is your greatest hope? Your deepest longing? Is it for
Christ to return? Be honest. That's not always at the top of
your list. The reason you are not eagerly waiting for Jesus is
because you either misunderstand his second coming and/or
love the world more than your King and his kingdom.

The return of Jesus is the finale of our salvation. It is the
climax of our redemption. For when he returns we are raised
and made like Jesus in perfected humanity, and sin and death
are finally vanquished and cast away forever. Those who
long to be entirely free from sin, evil, oppression, injustice,
and want to experience the fullness of God and his creation
without such hindrances, long for Christ's return. Those who
hate sin and love righteousness wait with eagerness for the
second coming. You misunderstand it if you think of it as an
interruption to your plans.

Setting your hope fully on the grace to be experienced
at the return of Jesus is not to deny the legitimacy of your
desire for marriage, children, or grandchildren. There are

many good things in life that you desire, and yet the return of Jesus can feel like an interruption to these things. After all, what should you desire more, for Christ to return now or for your friend to believe the gospel first? I think it is fair to say you should want your friend to trust Christ before the second coming or death. But to say that Jesus' return is our greatest hope means that his manifested glory and the end of sin is our greatest need.

In this life, as you work for the glory of Jesus and the good of others, you should do so with an eye to his return. It will lead to earnestness and create an urgency in your life to make the most of all your days.

PART TWO
THE GOSPEL AND OTHERS

14

STOP JUDGING

*Judge not, that you be not judged. For with the judgment
you pronounce you will be judged, and with the measure
you use it will be measured to you.
Why do you see the speck that is in your brother's eye,
but do not notice the log that is in your own eye?
Or how can you say to your brother, "Let me take the speck
out of your eye," when there is the log in your own eye?
You hypocrite, first take the log out of your own eye, and then
you will see clearly to take the speck out of your brother's eye.*

MATTHEW 7:1–5

Dear Self,

Stop judging. That's easy to say but not so easy to hear and
much harder to do. The truth is you won't stop judging
others until you stop seeing yourself as a measure of righteousness. I know, you are resistant to the idea that you are
self-righteous (which itself is a self-righteous response), but
you can be overly critical of some, while others seem to get
a pass.

The command to "judge not" is not a call to stop honest
evaluations about others but to cease the hypercritical
and condemning attitude that characterizes some of your
thoughts, words, and actions. Jesus tells you not to judge this
way because the world needs to see true judgment and real

mercy. What it knows of judgment is severe and unrighteous. What it knows of mercy is a permissive, "it's-all-good" attitude of tolerance or license.

Jesus tells you that this corrupt kind of judgment has no place in the life of his followers, as it does not complement the soul that has been shown mercy. You of all people know what it means to be extended mercy instead of judgment. Your experience of the gospel should compel you to demonstrate the gospel by living out the principles inherent in it.

Are you merciful, compassionate, and forgiving, or do you gravitate toward giving people what you believe they deserve? How do you receive people who are hostile to the gospel? How do you speak to or of people who are your social/political opposite? Here's a good test for yourself—how do you tip servers at a restaurant? Not just the good servers but even the bad ones. Have you considered that tipping generously, even if the service is bad, is a demonstration of grace that is not likely to be lost on the server? Stop judging. Let the gospel compel you to live by grace and demonstrate it to those around you.

15

STOP PRETENDING

. . . that we may be mutually encouraged by each other's faith,
both yours and mine.

ROMANS 1:12

Dear Self,

Like everyone else, you are pretty good at pretending. It is not malicious, but you can put on a good face when in reality things are not that good. You want to appear strong even when you are weak, or you at least do not want to appear weak. This superficial persona is the front of pride that only encourages the sin to continue in yourself, and it ultimately robs you of gospel influence—the kind of influence Paul had with the church in Rome, and they had with him.

When you pretend, you lose gospel influence in two ways—inwardly and outwardly. You lose the inward influence of the gospel in that you are not honest with others and deny them the opportunity to speak into your life. When you lack transparency, people are left without the opportunity to encourage you where you need it most. For example, sometimes you become anxious, but you have a good poker face. So you hold it together on the surface, but underneath it all you are in trouble. You need to tell the truth about what you are going through, and you need someone to tell you the truth of God. You need to hear of God's sovereign and good plan for the lives of those who love him, and how this is rooted in the gospel. You need to see the strong faith of others so that you can persevere through such times of anxiety and fear. You pretend to protect yourself but wind up sabotaging your own spiritual life by not being real. And you aren't hurting only yourself by pretending.

You lose outward influence of the gospel in the lives of others because you can't offer them anything that is real. Your best resource for speaking into others' lives is from what God is doing in you, the fruit that God is producing in you. But the fruit you want others to see is plastic. It is believable from a distance, but it nourishes no one. It is not real.

Know this—it is the gospel that allows you to be real. It admits us all as sinners and establishes us all as saints. Your local church is the only place where this reality, and not pretending, can be the culture of gathered community. Be real. Admit where you are and what you are. This will allow others to minister to you, and you to minister to others.

16

LOVE YOUR WIFE

Husbands, love your wives, as Christ loved the church and
gave himself up for her, that he might sanctify her,
having cleansed her by the washing of water with the word,
so that he might present the church to himself in splendor,
without spot or wrinkle or any such thing, that she might be
holy and without blemish.

EPHESIANS 5:25–27

Dear Self,

It is your calling and privilege to model Christ as husband to your wife through sacrifice and service. You are familiar enough with this passage to quote it and talk about it, but what counts is living it. Don't you know Jesus? Haven't you learned from him what love, sacrifice, and service look like? If so, you should be ready and eager to demonstrate this to your wife, because grace gives birth to grace. Because you know and follow Jesus, you are ready to truly love your wife.

That doesn't mean love is easy. It isn't. This is why it must be commanded and why you must be reminded. And consider this calling. You must not only have warm affection for your wife, you must love her as Christ loves the church. This is a sacrificial love—one that denies self and seeks the good of his bride.

I know that you say you would die for your wife, and I

believe you. But if that is true, why won't you let go of self-interests on her behalf? If you love her, and would lay down your life for her, why can't you lay down the remote control in order to give her your attention? Do you serve her and seek her betterment? Do you seek her growth in grace? Consider this: your calling is not only to care and provide for her in a general sense, but to seek her spiritual beautification. And this is primarily done as you model Christ to her as husband. No one else can do this for her; it is your calling alone.

You should seek to be the brightest representation of Jesus she sees, as you represent Christ as Savior and servant to her. That would look like seeking her out when you get home from work, instead of seeking solace for yourself. It means affirming her calling and gifts, listening to her, speaking words of encouragement to her, and at all times working for her good. Jesus loves you this way, and in like manner you are called to love your wife.

17

LOVE YOUR HUSBAND

Wives, submit to your own husbands, as to the Lord.
For the husband is the head of the wife even as Christ is the head of
the church, his body, and is himself its Savior.
Now as the church submits to Christ, so also wives should submit in
everything to their husbands.

EPHESIANS 5:22–24

Dear Self,

It is your calling and privilege to represent Christ to your husband in a way that he will see in no one else. You are called to submit to his godly leadership, support him in his leadership, and help him become what God desires.

Your occasional thoughts of the smallness of this calling demonstrate that you have not yet grasped the beauty of being your husband's "help-mate." Thinking of yourself as your husband's "helper" is not demeaning or small. It is actually a glorious position, and one that Jesus himself knew well.

Before his ascension, Jesus told his followers that he would "give you another helper." (John 14:16). He spoke of the Holy Spirit, but do not miss the point that the Holy Spirit is "another helper"—one like Jesus. Jesus did not have a problem thinking of himself as a helper, or even a helper to sinful men. This was his calling, the reason he was sent by the Father—to serve, help, and save sinners. Being considered the help of your husband means that he cannot succeed without you. He needs you to help him become the man God has designed him to be. Your role is reflected beautifully in the gospel, and you get to represent Jesus as "helper" to your husband in a way that no other person will, for no one else is called to this position.

Jesus modeled perfect submission to the Father, and it was in no way placing him in a place of lesser honor or glory. The Father and the Son are one, and yet one submits to the other. You are called to love your husband and represent Christ and the gospel to him. This means praising his hard work and expressing thanks for his working to provide for his family. It means doing him good and not evil (Prov. 31:12) and speaking honorably of him in public.

18

HONOR YOUR PARENTS

Children, obey your parents in the Lord, for this is right.
"Honor your father and mother"
(this is the first commandment with a promise),
"that it may go well with you and that you may live long
in the land."

EPHESIANS 6:1–3

Dear Self,

It is your privilege to exemplify Jesus as the submissive son to your parents through honor and obedience, yet you do not really think of it in this way. You see obedience to your parents as an empty kind of law keeping. Their rules feel arbitrary, and compliance seems pointless and unfulfilling. But you must remember three things—your calling, your good, and the example of Jesus.

Your calling as a child is to honor and obey your parents. This is not just because your parents have rules that must be followed, but that God calls you to live righteously by respecting your parents. And this calling to honor your parents ultimately works out for your good. There is a promise from God that assures you that as you learn and practice honoring and obeying your parents, you will find blessing. This may come in the form of protection or happiness, but it will always produce the fruit of godliness.

But it is the model of Jesus that will be most persuasive to you. For he knows better than anyone what it means to obey his Father, even when the task set before him is overwhelming. Jesus was perfectly submissive to the Father and was obedient to the good will of his Father even to the point of death. And such submission and obedience was not done merely to serve as an example, but to accomplish salvation for all who believe.

Where you have failed to honor and obey your parents, Jesus fulfilled the law by honoring both his earthly parents and ultimately his Father in heaven. This is your gospel hope. Jesus has showed you the way by accomplishing your salvation. And in his saving work, you not only find the way to follow, you also find the grace to empower such obedience.

And so here, you get to represent Jesus to your parents as the obedient son. Have you considered your calling in that light? You represent the Savior to your parents by honoring them. Fulfill your calling by following Jesus.

19

SOW GRACE

Whoever sows injustice will reap calamity,
and the rod of his fury will fail.
Whoever has a bountiful eye will be blessed,
for he shares his bread with the poor.

PROVERBS 22:8–9

Dear Self,

You should be sowing more grace. You should be more generous with your time, money, and gifts. The people around you, especially those who are unfriendly or even cross, need grace. Consider how you often give what you think is justice—that is, what you think people deserve. You tip less for bad service, ignore people who have snubbed you, or sigh and roll your eyes at the person taking up too much space at the coffeehouse. You may not be doing evil, but you are not doing good.

Ask yourself, "Am I known as a person of grace or a person of karma? Do people see in me the principle of 'you get what you deserve,' or 'what goes around comes around'?" If this is true of you, then people won't see Christ in you but will get a good dose of false religion. Such principles are already commonly understood in our culture, but the gospel principle of giving the good another does not deserve—that is different.

God calls you to love justice and demonstrate mercy.

Jesus commanded his followers to live generously and offer grace even to their enemies. Why are you offering less to those around you—to those God has sent you to as his ambassador? Perhaps because it is easier to aim at what you call justice? But such feelings are self-righteous, and acting as judge only feeds your ego. You were not made for this; you were made for the glory of God and the good of others.

What you need to consider therefore is that God commands you to live graciously because he is gracious. He commands you to be patient and merciful because such things find their beginning in him. And you not only know him, but you know his grace. God has extended mercy to you, blessing and forgiving you when you deserved much less. As a child of God, represent your Father well by showing grace. Sow it.

20

FORGIVE

*Put on then, as God's chosen ones, holy and beloved, compassionate
hearts, kindness, humility, meekness, and patience,
bearing with one another and,
if one has a complaint against another,
forgiving each other; as the Lord has forgiven you,
so you also must forgive.*

COLOSSIANS 3:12–13

Dear Self,

You need to forgive. You need to. You've heard people say
that not forgiving someone does more damage to themselves
than to the offender. You believe this is probably true, but
your need to forgive others goes beyond the good that you
experience from the act. You need to forgive others because
God in Jesus Christ has forgiven you. Your infinitely holy and
just Maker has not held your sins against you, but instead
has held them against his Son on the cross. Your faith rests
squarely on this act of substitution.

Your refusal to forgive one who has sinned against you
is a manifestation of hypocrisy—a telltale sign that either
you have not experienced God's forgiving grace, or that you
take such grace for granted. Why do you withhold what has
been given so freely to you? Have your offenders done worse
than you? Are their crimes against you more severe than your

crimes against God and others? When you refuse to forgive, it can only mean that you have not yet come to understand forgiveness, or you have been taking it for granted and have not yet sufficiently learned from it.

You need to forgive to make much of Jesus and his gospel. This is the real reason to extend forgiveness to the undeserving. You need to forgive not only so that you will find freedom, not only to extend kindness to others, but because in doing so you exalt Jesus and the salvation he offers to all who believe. Forgiveness points us all back to our greatest need—reconciliation to God by way of his own work.

Look, you can forgive. This is where you sometimes get stuck. You think it impossible. You have said to yourself, "I just can't forgive him." While forgiveness is never easy, it is also never impossible—not for those who have been saved by the grace of God. For the grace of salvation not only secures your forgiveness and models it for you, but it also empowers forgiveness by giving you a new heart and spirit.

You can forgive because you learned it in the gospel. This is the heart of the good news, that God forgives those who have sinned against him. You can forgive those who take what is yours, tempt you to fail, and taunt you for your faith—for these are your sins as well, and God has forgiven you. You can forgive those who have ignored, slighted, and hurt you because God has forgiven you of these very sins, and with that forgiveness he has given you a heart that longs to forgive. The gospel compels you to forgive, and it enables you to do so.

Give yourself to meditation on the cross; learn forgiveness, and walk in it.

21

INITIATE

*Go therefore and make disciples of all nations, baptizing them in
the name of the Father and of the Son and of the Holy Spirit,
teaching them to observe all that I have commanded you.
And behold, I am with you always, to the end of the age.*

MATTHEW 28:19–20

Dear Self,

You are familiar with these verses, and you tend to focus on
the command to "make disciples," which is only appropriate.
But consider for a moment this assumed idea of "going."
Disciples are made as you are going.

If you want to be useful to God, you will need to be
the person who moves first. You have to take the initiative
to move toward the people God has put into your life and
the people God has sent you to. Most will not come to your
church's worship gathering, most will not seek out your
advice, and most will not strike up a conversation with you.
You will have to go to them.

Your reasons for not initiating are legion. You do not
want to be that intrusive person who invites himself into
someone else's life. You do not want to be rejected. You want
things to happen naturally, and "initiating" sounds like a
sales pitch. Yet, the assumption is that as a disciple you are
already going—taking the first steps to reach out to those

around you. What you are neglecting is the normative behavior of disciples.

God has placed you in a unique context and equipped you in a unique way to be the one who reaches out to those in need—this means those who need encouragement as well as those who need correction. And this includes those who do not know Jesus, as well as his disciples, those who are apparently healthy, and those who are obviously hurting. You will have more opportunities to initiate than you can take, but you are likely to take fewer than you should.

Look around yourself. God is giving you chances to act. He has put people near you who need your help financially, your time relationally, and your words of bold encouragement and gentle rebuke. The opportunities are always there, but they are difficult to see if you are too focused on yourself. You must take the time to be truly present where God has put you. Begin to think of others as they really are—men and women in need of grace.

What will compel you to take the first step toward those around you in need? The deepness of their need? The desperateness of their situation? Perhaps it will be an understanding of what you have received from others who have been faithful to God and have taken the initiative with you, to help you see the truth, know Christ, grow in grace, and persevere through difficulty. Or maybe it will be that God not only commands you to do this but empowers you to do it, as well. Wherever you are, today you should be the first to move. Initiate for the glory of God and the good of those around you.

Read the rest of this book!

22

WELCOME

Contribute to the needs of the saints and seek to show hospitality.
ROMANS 12:13

Do not neglect to show hospitality to strangers.
HEBREWS 13:2

Dear Self,

Hospitality is not the quaint, fictional, domestic chore of stay-at-home TV moms. It is, in fact, the will of God for you. God commands you to be hospitable. This, like all of God's law, is not arbitrary. He does not just think of things to keep you busy. He calls you to be hospitable because he himself is a welcomer of strangers and loves the sojourner. Jesus is one who ate with sinners and welcomed the lost into his own life, and he calls you to follow him in his example of hospitality.

Throughout history, God has called his people to welcome outsiders into their cities, homes, and lives. Israel was commanded to practice hospitality with their Jewish neighbors, but also to welcome, care for, and bless those who visited their cities. Likewise, the church is also commanded to welcome both believers and unbelievers.

The most practical way in which you should be practicing hospitality is inviting people into your home in order to bless them. It is more than supplying dinner or dessert, but a way of caring for people. Hospitality can provide the context in which you discover the needs of others and can develop ways of meeting those needs. But at the very least, you can care for people by providing them with authentic relationships and community in the context of your own home.

The most basic idea behind hospitality is to care for outsiders in a way that you would care for insiders. You welcome them. So, when was the last time you invited outsiders into your home? Into your busy life? Outsiders are not those close to you but those who are not yet a part of your life. This includes people at church you have not taken the time to meet as well as your neighbors and coworkers you do not yet know. They may be outside or inside the kingdom, but they are currently outside of your ministry influence.

Of course there is no better picture of hospitality than what we find in the gospel, for in the gospel God calls those who were not his people, "My people." By faith we are orphans who have been adopted into God's family, made coheirs with Christ, and are promised a place at his table in the kingdom to come. God has accepted you and welcomed you in Christ. You know what it is to be an outsider and yet received as an insider, so you should be ready to show others what that kind of grace looks like on a smaller scale in your home.

23

LISTEN TO OTHERS

*Take care, brothers, lest there be in any of you an evil,
unbelieving heart, leading you to fall away from the living God.
But exhort one another every day, as long as it is called "today,"
that none of you may be hardened by the deceitfulness of sin.*

HEBREWS 3:12–13

Dear Self,

God has put certain people in your life and will lead others across your path to encourage and correct you. The problem is that much of the time you just are not listening. You like to think of yourself as a listener because you so desperately want God to speak into your life and provide wisdom. You think of yourself as open and willing to heed God's wisdom. You think you are ready to move once God provides direction, but you expect God to make this known to you privately—perhaps while you're reading Scripture or praying—without the involvement of others.

What you fail to realize is that one of the primary ways in which God will answer your prayer for wisdom is by speaking to you through other people. While God can reveal himself in dramatic visions and dreams, his common means of providing wisdom and guidance to his people is through his people as they exhort one another in the Word.

You want God to speak, but are you willing to hear him

speak to you through others? Make no mistake about it—you need to hear from others for your own progress in the faith. The author of Hebrews says that through mutual exhortation believers are protected from the hardening influences of sin.

Make no mistake about it—you need to listen to others, because otherwise, sin begins to petrify your heart. This means you become less sensitive to the leading of the Holy Spirit and increasingly insensitive to the ugliness of your own corruption. A petrified heart is an ugly irony because it is like a returning to the heart of stone God once removed and replaced with a heart of flesh. To work against this hardening, God calls you to be in and listen to the Christian community. Proverbs tells us there are answers to be found in the counsel of friends (Prov. 24:6). What this implies is that you need the local church, and you need to see the body of Christ as the people God brings into your life to learn from.

So the local church must be more than a weekly event. It needs to be your covenant community and extended family who have the right and privilege to exhort you—to speak into your life when you need it most. From words of encouragement to gentle but needed rebuke, the words of wisdom and insight are all around you. Are you listening?

24

SPEAK TO OTHERS

Take care, brothers, lest there be in any of you an evil,
unbelieving heart, leading you to fall away from the living God.
But exhort one another every day, as long as it is called "today,"
that none of you may be hardened by the deceitfulness of sin.

HEBREWS 3:12–13

Dear Self,

Are you connected to others in such a way that affords you opportunities to speak into their lives? Just as God has put people near you to speak to you for your God, so he has intended to use you to speak words of grace to others. The questions are—are you connected, and are you speaking?

It is not enough to just be around others, maintaining politeness and pleasantries. You must be connected to others more deeply, in true community, where you are doing life together and pursuing the same purpose together. And even then, you are not there merely to receive direction, encouragement, and comfort. God wants you there to offer these things to others as well. You will be called to do more than be aware of their needs and pray for them. That much is relatively easy. At times you will need to open your mouth and speak. And this can only happen in the context of community.

At times you feel as if you have little to say, or that your words are too simple and not deep enough. But when you doubt that you have anything to offer, you question God's ability to use you beyond your own weakness. Your usefulness in the lives of others is not dependent on your intellectual or creative abilities, though God will use your talents whatever they are. Your usefulness to God and his people is connected with your dependence on God and his Word and your love for his people.

The people around you need to hear from you. Share God's Word with those who need to hear it.

25

YOU CAN'T MAKE IT ALONE

Take care, brothers, lest there be in any of you an evil,
unbelieving heart, leading you to fall away from the living God.
But exhort one another every day, as long as it is called "today,"
that none of you may be hardened by the deceitfulness of sin.

HEBREWS 3:12–13

Dear Self,

Let me be direct. You are not strong enough, or spiritual enough to successfully follow Jesus and be faithful to his mission on your own. The words of God recorded in Genesis, "It is not good for man to be alone," speak not only to the issue of marriage but also to a very basic need all people have. We are created by God to dwell in community. You have been considering your need to both hear and speak biblical exhortation in community, but you also need to consider that the mission of Jesus, which you have been called to participate in, is carried out only through the church.

Consider the mission of the church: "Go therefore and make disciples of all nations, baptizing them in the name of the Father and of the Son and of the Holy Spirit, teaching them to observe all that I have commanded you" (Matt. 28:19–20). The mission is to make disciples; and to make disciples, one must be a disciple. In both of these callings the church is essential to the work.

To be a disciple of Jesus you must belong to and work with, for, and through the local church. You need the strengthening, encouragement, and reproof that only the church can give, and you need the church to be faithful to the command of Jesus. God calls his followers to live in community together, loving, serving, sharing, and discipling one another. The church, for all of its faults, is essentially connected to God's mission and our spiritual life. You simply cannot survive spiritually on a weekly worship service, podcasts, and books. You need the community more than you probably realize. You can't make it alone; nor can anyone else.

26
LIVE SHORT

Christ will be honored in my body,
whether by life or by death.
For to me to live is Christ, and to die is gain.
If I am to live in the flesh, that means fruitful labor for me.
Yet which I shall choose I cannot tell.
I am hard pressed between the two. My desire is to depart
and be with Christ, for that is far better.
But to remain in the flesh is more necessary on your account.
Convinced of this, I know that I will remain
and continue with you all,
for your progress and joy in the faith,
so that in me you may have ample cause to glory in Christ Jesus,
because of my coming to you again.

PHILIPPIANS 1:20–26

Dear Self,

The call to live every day as your last is not anything new. You've heard it quite a bit, and you even "amen" the sentiment. But why haven't you given it more thought? The call to live today as if it were your last is not a romantic notion of living life to the fullest. It is a call to recognize that God is sovereign and has ordered your days from beginning to end. It is to recognize that God has given you today but has not promised you tomorrow. What this means, then, is that you are a fool if you presume that you have tomorrow while taking for granted the grace you have today.

Consider that God has ordered your days. He has given you a certain number of days to use for his glory and the good of those around you. What are you doing with the time you have? Remember, we are not talking about the time you think you have, but the time you actually have. If you knew for certain that this was in fact the last day of your life, what would you do? Would you hole up in your house, kneeling, repenting for all the sin you have neglected? Would you run to every friend and relative who does not know Christ and encourage them to repent and believe the gospel? But while today could be your last, you do not know it, so the best course of action is simply to be faithful to the things God has called you to this day, for it could be your last. Will you love your spouse? Talk with your kids? Do your best at your place of employment? Pray and seek God with earnestness and sincerity?

You see, you have to make the most, not just of the day as a whole, but of all of the parts that make up that day. That is your responsibility. Live short; live with urgency. This is the natural outworking of truly embracing our chief end of glorifying God and enjoying him forever.

27
LIVE LONG

Christ will be honored in my body,
whether by life or by death.
For to me to live is Christ, and to die is gain.
If I am to live in the flesh, that means fruitful labor for me.
Yet which I shall choose I cannot tell.
I am hard pressed between the two. My desire is to depart
and be with Christ, for that is far better.
But to remain in the flesh is more necessary on your account.
Convinced of this, I know that I will remain
and continue with you all,
for your progress and joy in the faith,
so that in me you may have ample cause to glory in Christ Jesus,
because of my coming to you again.
PHILIPPIANS 1:20–26

Dear Self,

As you consider the need to live urgently in the now, making the most of the day God has given you, you must still look ahead and plan for the future. You need to live long with the awareness that God may have years ahead planned for you. While you shouldn't presume on the grace of God to give you tomorrow, it is not foolish to work today in anticipation of tomorrow. However, tomorrow can only be prepared for by making the most of today. So while you make the most of the day God has given you, it is important to look ahead to where your day might lead you and others down the road. You are never just living for the moment. You are living for eternity, and your life has the potential to prove fruitful not only for yourself, but also for many others.

To live long means that you are thinking into the future for the well-being of yourself and others. It is good to ask if you have a plan in place to grow your family in the faith, preparing them for the potential hardships ahead that you are most likely to lead them through. I'm not saying you need to act like a business and have a five-year plan, but it is certainly good to think through where you would like you and your family to be five or ten years down the road, and then begin working toward that goal.

Consider your calling, and then determine what it means for you, as a Christian, to fulfill your calling in such a way that will glorify God, serve his mission, and demonstrate grace to the world.

PART THREE
THE GOSPEL AND YOU

28

HATE WELL

The fear of the LORD is hatred of evil.
Pride and arrogance and the way of evil
and perverted speech I hate.

PROVERBS 8:13

Dear Self,

In all your longing to love as Christ loved, you sometimes forget that true love for one thing will, or at least should, produce a hatred for whatever stands against it. Do not neglect cultivating hatred, an intense hatred, for the right things. Authentic love and zeal for God will produce abhorrence for all that stands opposed to him and his purposes. Genuine love for your neighbor will produce within you antipathy toward all that robs him of his dignity or leads her away from God.

Do you hate pride and arrogance? Injustice and the way of evil? Hurtful speech? Do false gospels and false teachers create a holy hostility in you? Do you hate works-righteousness and the false promise of peace with God through performance? I hope you do.

And what about your own sin? Do you see it? Is it ever before your eyes? Do you really hate it for what it is, or do you simply dislike its unpleasant consequences? If you hate your sin only because of the pain it has caused you in this life, then your hatred stems from self-love and does not come from a burning love for God.

At times you have wondered why you are so complacent, unmoved. You have grown frustrated with your lack of progress in the faith. It may be because you lack true and balanced passion—love and hatred. One will move you to recoil from sin, and the other will move you to hold on to Jesus.

Consider the apostle Paul, who wrestled with the ugly reality of sin in his life (Rom. 7:7–25). Paul's hatred for sin and love for the Savior led him to war against the flesh and to hope in Jesus. And while he was resigned to the hard truth that this side of the resurrection he was shackled to the corrupting influence and presence of sin, his confidence was always grounded in the unchanging love and abounding grace of God. This is why Paul could write, "Wretched man that I am! Who will deliver me from this body of death? Thanks be to God through Jesus Christ our Lord! So then, I myself serve the law of God with my mind, but with my flesh I serve the law of sin. There is therefore now no condemnation for those who are in Christ Jesus." (Rom. 7:24–8:1)

If you are following Jesus, cherishing the gospel, and loving God and neighbor, then you will hate well. If you do not hate evil, you will find yourself more susceptible to temptation, slower to respond to corruption, and unmotivated to contend for the faith. Hate is a real part of your faith—don't forget it.

29

KEEP YOUR HEART

Keep your heart with all vigilance,
for from it flow the springs of life.

PROVERBS 4:23

Dear Self,

You work at keeping your conduct in line, and you work at maintaining a good reputation, but you don't work enough at keeping your heart. The problem with this is unless you learn to keep your heart, your conduct and reputation will be of little value and may come crashing down in times of weakness.

The call to keep your heart is a call to work on your life internally, not merely externally. The latter is easy; the former is much harder and more complicated. The religious or moral person will focus on the external and maintain good appearances, but it may have little to nothing to do with the heart. God is first and foremost concerned with your heart, for when you are keeping your heart, the rest of life follows.

To keep your heart means that your focus and work is on maintaining communion with God and pursuing the transformation that only God can accomplish in you. It is not performance-based religion, nor the moral improvement of your life, but the ongoing work of cultivating love for God and hatred for sin. It is the unending effort of guarding ourselves against idols while resting in the promises of the gospel.

To keep your heart is your primary business as a Christian, and it cannot be done with passing interest or any small amount of energy. It requires the consistent use of all the means of grace. You must make the most of worship, Scripture, prayer, and the church gathered in all its forms with an aim at keeping your heart and growing in grace. If you are doing anything less than this, you are keeping up appearances but not your heart. And you know that the heart is what God is primarily interested in (Ps. 51:16–17)—hearts that are broken over sin, healed by God's forgiving grace, and consequently filled with love for our Redeemer God.

30

REPENT

For godly grief produces a repentance that leads to
salvation without regret.
2 CORINTHIANS 7:10

Dear Self,

You will never be done with repentance—at least, not until death or Christ's return. While it is something you should be doing frequently, it is not something you just "get used to." Repentance requires a daily intentionality. And let's be honest; you will have more to repent of by the end of the day than you can possibly remember. So, where should you start? The big picture is that repentance is both an attitude and an action. It is more than being sorry for sin, and it is more than cutting out a bad habit.

It will be helpful to think of repentance in three parts: revulsion, resolution, and repetition. Revulsion is finding something offensive or distasteful. In this case, it is seeing the heinousness of sin and pulling back from it. Sin, your sin in particular, should make you recoil. Yet, because you are so familiar and comfortable with your sin, you hardly even blush at most of it. Revulsion will come only when you see the holy, just, and good character of God in contrast to yourself. Until you understand that your sin, all of it, is a self-destructive rebellion against God that betrays your purpose and denies his worthiness, you will not experience revulsion.

Resolution is purposing to walk in righteousness, delighting in God's law, laying off the old self, and walking in newness of life. Repentance is more than feeling sorry for what you are and have done. It is having the resolve to live for the glory and pleasure of God.

Repetition is the ongoing nature of this work. Without repetition, it is all for nothing, for as long as you continue to sin, you need to repent. If your repentance is not continual, it means, at the very least, that you are simply choosing some sins to deal with, while ignoring others. This is likely to lead to a sense of pride that gives you confidence that you have overcome your sins and have "arrived," while in reality, you have only become a bit more religious.

The deepness and consistency of your repenting will have a direct impact on the liveliness of your faith and the brightness of your confidence. This is not because you repent so well, but because in repenting you know the darkness and trouble of your own sin, and the great work of grace in Jesus that overcomes it all.

31
DIE TO SIN

He himself bore our sins in his body on the tree, that we might die to
sin and live to righteousness. By his wounds you have been healed.
For you were straying like sheep, but have now returned to the
Shepherd and Overseer of your souls.

1 PETER 2:24–25

Dear Self,

Yes, Jesus died as a substitute for sinners, and that work is
your hope of salvation. But Jesus did not die only to justify
the wicked. His death is also designed to lead you in your
own daily dying and living.

Peter says that Jesus died for our sins so that we would
die to our sins. Jesus died for our sins by suffering the wrath
of God in the place of sinners. By his wounds we are healed.
Through the suffering of the righteous one, the wicked are
justified. You, Christian, are justified. But his death should
lead you in dying, as well.

You die to your sins and live to righteousness through
the ongoing work of faith and repentance. To die to sin is
to deny its influence and to recognize that sin is powerless
over you. It means that you recognize your corruption and
identify your temptations while resting in the deliverance
God has provided through the sacrifice of Jesus. You are no
longer a slave, and sin is your master no more. As you die to

sin (recognizing and living in the reality that Jesus has set you free) you can live to righteousness. To live to righteousness is to follow Christ in holiness and to grow in grace.

What all this means is that the death of Jesus is not just what cleanses you of guilt, but it is also the means by which you experience transformation. Your progress in the faith, your sanctification, is not a result of will power or education but the consequence of Christ's atoning work. That is your confidence and hope. You can die to sin because he has died for your sin. You can live unto righteousness because Jesus has risen from the dead and in him you are now truly alive! Today is a day to die and to live.

32

KILL YOUR SIN

For if you live according to the flesh you will die,
but if by the Spirit you
put to death the deeds of the body, you will live.

ROMANS 8:13

Dear Self,

You seem to think that your sins will somehow die of old age. It's as if you believe you can wait them out, and they will eventually grow weak and fail. But the truth is your sin ages more like an oak tree. If you aren't chopping it down, its roots are growing deeper, and its branches are growing stronger.

In other words, your sin will not just go away. You are called to aggressively seek sin's destruction—to kill it. But even when you understand this, it is more complicated than plotting its murder, for the act of killing sin is a slow, continuous process that runs the span of your life. And if you are not putting sin to death, then you will find that it is seeking your destruction. As John Owen said, "Be killing sin or it will be killing you."

Killing sin isn't merely the cutting of branches but a striking at the root. This means you need to do more than recognize your sin of impatience; you must seek to know how this branch of sin is connected to the root of pride. From there you can get to work. But the work of killing sin is not moral improvement or personal reformation. It is the Holy Spirit empowered spiritual war against all forms of corruption that would lead you away from the gospel. Sin and temptation lead you away from the gospel by telling you that you can find greater fulfillment and satisfaction in something other than Jesus. Your sinful actions always reflect the battle within you over your allegiance.

What this means is that the true nature of spiritual warfare is a fight against indwelling sin, and that the only success you can have in that fight is through the power of God's Spirit. And how is it that you and the Spirit can work together? How is it that the Holy Spirit has come to dwell in you? The answer is found in the gospel. God justifies the sinner, gives him the Spirit, and sanctifies him in the truth by the Spirit. Your hope in this war against sin is outside of yourself in God. In the end, you are called to kill sin because it seeks to lead you away from the hope of the gospel, and you are able to kill sin because of the hope of the gospel.

33

REBOUND

I have blotted out your transgressions like a cloud
and your sins like mist;
return to me, for I have redeemed you.

ISAIAH 44:22

Dear Self,

Too often you let your sin anchor you in place. You do not move beyond it or even see beyond it. In some cases this turns into a form of self-pity when you are grieved by your sin, but not so deeply that you are moved to repent and discover joy in your salvation. You feel defeated, victimized, and beyond help. In some ways this actually relieves you of a sense of responsibility. After all, what could you have done? Temptation always seems to get the best of you. Your sin appears overwhelming while the grace of God seems small, and instead of rising up in the grace God provides to return to him again, you remain in place feeling sorry for yourself.

Sometimes this self-pity morphs into that guilt-penance in which the worse you feel about yourself and your situation, the more ready you feel to approach God again—not because of his grace but because of your contrition. So you wind up feeling stuck and unable to seek God, or you find that you can only return to him after you have sufficiently beaten yourself up spiritually.

But in the gospel Jesus says, "Come to me." Jesus came to save sinners, to forgive the guilty, and to cleanse the corrupt. This means the painful presence of sin in your life should not be an occasion of remaining distant from God but another reason to draw near. Your unrighteousness is not a reason to run from God but a reason to run to God. Only in the Son will you find cleansing, healing, and restoration, and always in him do you find acceptance.

You can, and must, return to God daily. His promise is that he will receive you as you come—in faith, not in moral purity. This is what gospel confidence looks like. It is not an insincere approach to God that dismisses our corruption while presuming on his grace, but a heartfelt dependency on the grace of Christ to make us acceptable at all times. Gospel confidence is not found in our best religious performance, be it guilt-penance or law keeping, but in the merit and mercy of Jesus on our behalf.

Your sin is your own, and while it is a cause for mourning, it is never a cause to run from God. You must return to God, rebound from your sin, and seek God with grateful boldness.

34

YOU ARE PROUD

Clothe yourselves, all of you, with humility toward one another,
for "God opposes the proud but gives grace to the humble."

1 PETER 5:5

Dear Self,

You are proud, and what makes this so dangerous is that you don't realize just how proud you are. There are two reasons you see pride as a sin that isn't a real problem for you. One is that you are quick to compare yourself to the worst examples of proud men and women, and this gives you a sense of self-righteousness that comforts you. Comparatively, you believe you aren't "that bad." This makes little of a very serious sin problem.

You need to stop comparing yourself to others and begin considering the ways pride manifests itself in your life. You demonstrate the sin of pride whenever you put yourself before others. Your pride bubbles to the surface when you balk at the inconveniences of life. How dare something rebel against the egocentric universe you rule over? Pride lies behind every sin, for in the moment you choose it, you deny God and exalt yourself.

Pride is why you rage, lust, covet, steal, and lie. You do these things because you believe you deserve what you don't have. This kind of pride denies God and others the place they should have in your life.

The second reason you think pride isn't a serious issue for you is that you think so little of your talents and abilities. But poor self-esteem is not an indication of humility or meekness. In fact, it may be a disregarding of the gifts God has given you and a mocking of the work he is doing in your life. How does this connect to pride? Haven't you used this excuse of no ability and no talent to clear yourself of responsibility? Isn't it possible that you have used poor self-esteem as an excuse for doing nothing or as a means of saving face? Who could fault you when you don't claim to be good at anything? Make no mistake about it—you are proud!

What you need is a clear picture of God, yourself, and your hope; and this only comes through law and gospel. You must see yourself as you really are—creature, not Creator; sinful, not righteous; undeserving, not deserving; dependent, not independent; made for his glory, not for your own. And you must know God as holy, just, good, gracious, and merciful, who saves all who trust in him, and not in themselves. This is the theology that erodes pride, builds humility, and produces joy.

35

STOP COMPLAINING

Do all things without grumbling or questioning.

PHILIPPIANS 2:14

Dear Self,

Let's get something straight. You complain, and you know it. You complain in the car, in your home, at church, and about a number of different things. The problem with your complaining is that you do not see it as a problem. You view it as harmless venting. You believe you are just stating facts, that a certain circumstance is frustrating. Your justification of complaining is truly unfortunate, because it certainly bothers God. The reason you complain is the reason it is wrong.

You complain because you misunderstand (or just miss altogether) the grace you have received and the purposes of God in your life. You misunderstand the grace you have received by not recognizing it and receiving it with gratitude. Life, breath, and all of God's provisions for your life are acts of his kindness and are truly wonderful, and yet they all seem to disappear when the small inconveniences of life appear.

In most of your complaining you miss the good purposes of God for your life—purposes he has made clear. "God causes all things to work together for good to those who love God" (Rom. 8:28 NASB). This truth should remain a constant meditation, particularly in a world filled with frustration, frailty, and failure. Though we are not always aware of the particular ways in which God causes all things to work out for our good, we have this promise, and it should be enough to challenge and conquer our complaining spirit.

And no, you do not get a pass because you can handle the big problems in life with this promise but not the small ones. Perhaps when sickness, death, and affliction come into your life, you run to God and his promises and find comfort that gives peace and patience. Maybe it is just the small stuff that you sweat. So what is the big deal? Everything! In fact, your complaining about the small stuff is more dangerous than complaining about the big, because life is made up of the small stuff. Tragedies punctuate periods of your life, but it is the smaller inconveniences that make up the bulk of your existence, and this is what most people will see you handle. Those situations are the most obvious testing ground of your faith. If God's grace is big enough for you to handle the big problems, why isn't it enough for you to walk meekly through the smaller issues?

Perhaps the lesson is that you haven't driven the gospel deep enough into your heart and mind. Otherwise it would bear fruit precisely where you need it. Are you complaining today? Consider the grace of God in all of life, and in the gospel particularly. Be assured of his purpose in all things inconvenient and tragic, and you will find the cure for complaining.

36
KNOW YOUR IDOLS

Little children, keep yourselves from idols.

1 JOHN 5:21

Dear Self,

The call to keep one's self from idols is given to the church. This sounds strange, as you see yourself as a worshiper of God and not of strange deities. But there it is at the end of John's epistle. His last words in that letter to the church are, "Keep yourselves from idols." The warning isn't given to them because it wasn't a real danger or because there was an off chance someone might fall into idolatry. It was given because this is our root problem on any given day. It is what we, especially as followers of Jesus, must fight against.

Even when you know the dangers of idolatry and the command to keep yourself from idols, do you know what idols you need to keep yourself from? It is not enough to say that you will worship Christ alone and reject false gods. You must be able to recognize the form idolatry takes in your life.

Paul points out that covetousness itself is a form of idolatry (Col. 3:5), so you know that an idol does not need to take the shape of traditionally recognized gods. Rather, idolatry is the exaltation of anyone or anything above God. Covetousness is a form of idolatry because it is both the exaltation of the object desired as well as of yourself, while Christ is eclipsed by both.

Confronting your idols first requires you to identify them. This is a heart work that asks questions that will address heart issues. Where do your thoughts drift to and in what do they delight? What are you most afraid of? What is it that gives the greatest value to your life, without which life would be meaningless? Questions like these will help you identify your idols, which must then be confronted with the supremacy of Jesus and his gospel. Just as you are called by Jesus to daily deny yourself, take up your cross, and follow him, so are you called to keep yourself from idols.

37

THEOLOGY IS FOR WORSHIP

When Jesus had spoken these words, he lifted up his eyes to heaven,
and said, "Father, the hour has come; glorify your Son
that the Son may glorify you, since you have given him authority
over all flesh, to give eternal life to all whom you have given him.
And this is eternal life, that they know you the only true God,
and Jesus Christ whom you have sent."

JOHN 17:1–3

Dear Self,

You know you need to check yourself. Daily. Especially when it comes to your theology. Not only because there is always the danger of getting theology wrong, but also because of the danger of your theology hosting the parasite of pride. Pride can attach itself to your theology and feed off it to such a degree that you will believe it actually belongs there. This demonstrates a very basic problem in your doctrine; even if the propositions of your theology are correct, the end of theology is missed, for the end of theology is worship.

Good theology will always lead to humility and worship. It displays the greatness of God. It shows that he is transcendent, sovereign, holy, and good. It reflects the beauty of Jesus and the gospel, and the wonder of God's justice and mercy coming together in the life, death, and resurrection of Jesus. Good theology uncovers the truth about ourselves—that we are men and women made in God's image, who exist for his glory, but have turned inward and ugly through our own sin. Without the hope of the gospel we are objects of wrath and await destruction. But in Christ we are reconciled to God.

Humility is properly born out of this theology. In seeing the greatness of God and who we are as his creation, we become characterized by a spirit of growing awe, wonder, and meekness, and are drawn to worship. We can exalt and exult in the God who has not only made himself known but also invited us to draw near to him as he draws near to us. Developing a theology that leads to worship requires you to approach doctrine devotionally—that is with the aim of a life of worship devoted to a Person, not a principle. It means you will read Scripture, and even theology books, with the goal of knowing Christ deeply and making him known clearly.

38

WORSHIP OUT LOUD

Ascribe to the LORD, O heavenly beings,
ascribe to the LORD glory and strength.
Ascribe to the LORD the glory due his name;
worship the LORD in the splendor of holiness.

PSALM 29:1–2

Dear Self,

It's pretty clear that sometimes you think about gathered worship in the wrong way. So let's just clear up what it isn't. Gathering with the church for Word, sacrament, prayer, and song was not commanded by God to put "gas in your tank" for the rest of the week. You know it is not a show meant to entertain you, but it's also much more than a refresher. It is deeper than momentary inspiration, and it is bigger than simply "being fed."

Of course, gathering with the church and worshiping a risen Savior will feed, encourage, and equip you. It should also be one of the primary contexts in which God brings about real and lasting change in your life. Where else can you receive such concentrated doses of the gospel? However, this gathering does not exist only for your good. Its primary aim is the glory and pleasure of God.

Public worship is your response to the gospel, but it is a response meant to be expressed with other believers. It amounts to the collective offering of praise and adoration to God. You should think of worship as an opportunity to offer something to God, not just to receive something. You should come with the intention of offering your words, your mind, your heart, and your entire life to the God who has rescued you from sin, death, and hell itself. And when you gather for worship in this way, you can also come with the eager anticipation of grace from God. You will be convicted and encouraged, humbled and made strong by the Word and Spirit of God.

And one other thing—you should think of public worship as the pinnacle of the week. It is not the catalyst that gives movement to the other six days as much as it is the goal toward which you are working throughout the week. Your week should consist of days of private and family worship in which you are being prepared to meet with God as a church family.

Stop thinking so small when it comes to the church gathering for worship. It is for God's pleasure, your good, and the health of your church. Prepare for such a meeting with God today, and worship out loud with your brothers and sisters.

39

WORSHIP IN PRIVATE

O God, you are my God; earnestly I seek you;
my soul thirsts for you; my flesh faints for you,
as in a dry and weary land where there is no water.
So I have looked upon you in the sanctuary,
beholding your power and glory.

My soul will be satisfied as with fat and rich food,
and my mouth will praise you with joyful lips,
when I remember you upon my bed,
and meditate on you in the watches of the night.

PSALM 63:1–2, 5–6

Dear Self,

Gathered worship may be the pinnacle of the week when God's people worship out loud in public, but that gathering is fed by your ongoing private worship, which is much more than having a "quiet time."

Focused devotional exercises are important, but your tendency is to think that such spiritual discipline is the totality of private worship. The truth is that the whole of your life should be an ongoing act of worship. If your meditation on Scripture, prayer, and seeking of God is limited to a thirty-minute quiet time, you will wind up having a romantic experience in the morning and an atheistic experience throughout the rest of the day when life gets real.

It is a good thing to begin your day worshiping God in private through the intake of Scripture and the lifting up of prayer to God, but what begins your day should be carried throughout the remaining hours God gives you. Private worship is only valuable when you understand that it is not a thing you do in an hour, but the activity of the heart that exists in concentrated periods of devotional exercises and in the very ordinary moments of your days.

You should be connecting the needs, crises, and victories every day to spontaneous, if often inaudible, expressions of prayer and praise. You should be seeking God for wisdom and strength in the midst of your calling, whether that is in the home, at the office, or in the garage. The knowledge of God should lead you to experience the person of God where you are. You should be worshiping in private, and that includes time alone with God as well as working for his glory and pleasure in the vocational aspects of your life.

40

THEOLOGY TALKS

But you are a chosen race, a royal priesthood, a holy nation, a people
for his own possession, that you may proclaim
the excellencies of him who
called you out of darkness into his marvelous light.

1 PETER 2:9

Dear Self,

Your theology is not merely for your own personal interest or benefit. You do know what theology actually is, right? Theology literally means "words about God" or "God talk." Think about it this way. Theology is not meant merely to be known, but to be made known. This means the theology you have developed is not finished until it is articulated and spoken for others to hear. God has spoken in his Word. He has revealed himself there so that you could both know him and make him known. Theology talks.

You need to consider this: your theology—as tight as you think it is—is underdeveloped if you are not speaking it, sharing it. On a practical level this means you should be sharing the gospel with those God has sent you to. And for the record, the gospel itself is the climax of all theology. There is nothing deeper, more powerful, or more relevant to make known. If you are more excited about any facet of the truth of God other than the gospel, you have issues that need to be addressed. Yet, it is true that all theology is meant to be shared. The knowledge of God in all its detail is relevant to life, and we are either making the connection or neglecting the truth of God. As you consider yourself a theologian, be sure that you are not mute, or you have stopped short of becoming the theologian God delights in.

This does not require you to grab a bullhorn and soapbox and hit the street corner, but it does demand that you take the always bold and sometimes prophetic step of speaking to the people around you. At the very least you should look for opportunities to share what you are learning of God and his gospel so that it bears fruit in the lives of others. Do you find hope in his forgiveness? Strength from his Spirit and Word? Safety in his sovereign care and purposes? Comfort in his presence? How can you hold these things in? You are created in Christ Jesus to be known as one who proclaims his excellencies. Your theology must talk—first to yourself and then to others.

41

BE CAREFUL IN YOUR THEOLOGY

Keep a close watch on yourself and on the teaching.
Persist in this, for by so doing you will save both yourself
and your hearers.

1 TIMOTHY 4:16

Dear Self,

Your views of God and self are not small ideas of little consequence. You must carefully do the hard work of building a theology that reflects truth. Do not merely settle for the study you have already done. This is more than laziness; it is carelessness with the truth of God. What you have already accomplished is not sufficient to have arrived at a perfect "body of divinity." You need to continue to study and articulate the truth throughout your life. As one who believes that sin has corrupted every faculty of a man, you must acknowledge that if there is corruption in your heart and mind, there is probably some error in your doctrine as well.

Don't settle for the teaching of one teacher or system because you like the leadership there. And do not blindly embrace a tradition because you believe it is the simply the closest option out there to what the apostles gave us. While you will do well to listen carefully to those teachers who have gone before you, especially those teachers who consistently preached and taught the whole counsel of God, you must remain careful.

To be careful in your theological development is to be ultimately persuaded of the authority and the sufficiency of Scripture, as well as of the worthiness of God. If Scripture is the only perfect and certain Word from God, which alone is the flawless revelation of God, then read it, study it, and then articulate the truths it teaches carefully, so as not to misrepresent God or lead people away from the truth. You do not get to rest just because you believe you chose the right theological tribe. You must continue to exercise due diligence in your investigation and articulation of the truth. By it you will both know God and make him known, or you will misunderstand God and lead others into error.

42

DON'T BE A FAN BOY

For it has been reported to me by Chloe's people that there is
quarreling among you, my brothers.
What I mean is that each one of you says,
"I follow Paul," or "I follow Apollos," or "I follow Cephas,"
or "I follow Christ."
Is Christ divided? Was Paul crucified for you?
Or were you baptized in the name of Paul?
1 CORINTHIANS 1:11–13

Dear Self,

It is good to admire others who walk with God, serve as an example, and encourage you in the faith. But neither the world nor the church needs any more fan boys (and you can be a bit of a fan boy). What people need is humble, worshiping theologians who are more passionate for God and gospel than they are for personalities.

The difference between a fan boy and a humble, worshiping theologian is the direction of one's passions, the content of their convictions, and the source of their identity. The fan boy is passionate about a personality or movement, shares that person's convictions, and is careful to align himself with the right people for acceptance. It is not that the fan boy is out to deceive or pretend. He truly believes the personality or tribe is right. But instead of standing with such people and focusing intently on Jesus, he settles for spiritual tribalism and the cult of personality.

Let me be clear. Point to those who follow Christ well, but only to encourage others to see Christ more clearly. Link up with like-minded men and women who are serious about God, gospel, and mission, but fight the temptation to let the group be your passion rather than its reason for existence.

Don't be a fan boy. Be known as one who loves Jesus, the church, and the world. Be a person who knows the truth and makes it known, and who is willing not only to join with others for the cause of Christ and his kingdom, but is also willing to challenge that group when things get out of line.

43

WORK

Whatever you do, work heartily, as for the Lord and not for men,
knowing that from the Lord you will receive the inheritance
as your reward.
You are serving the Lord Christ.

COLOSSIANS 3:23–24

Dear Self,

You need to see all of life as spiritual, and your calling or employment as work for God regardless of pay, position, or its connection to the church. In other words, stop treating what you spend the bulk of your day engaged in as something divorced from God and his work in and through you.

Your work is one of the primary ways in which you will glorify God. For as you do it in faith, thankfulness, and godliness, you are serving God and reflecting his beauty to everyone around you.

Perhaps you struggle with wondering how your oh-so-ordinary and mundane work could glorify God, and maybe you even believe that translating the Bible into a language that has never read Scripture before is something that brings more glory to God than what you are doing. You think that way because you have not yet grasped that God is glorified by his people when his people are faithful to him.

Your calling is to be faithful to God where you are, and in doing this all work is sacred, spiritual, and worthy of your full attention and energy. When you get to work, you are not entering a secular environment as much as you are bringing the sacred into the world by following Christ wherever you are.

44

SUFFER WELL

We rejoice in our sufferings, knowing that suffering
produces endurance, and endurance produces character, and
character produces hope, and hope does not put us to shame,
because God's love has been poured into our hearts through
the Holy Spirit who has been given to us.

ROMANS 5:3–5

Dear Self,

God does not promise to rid your life of affliction and difficulty. He does, however, offer to give you the grace needed to suffer well, and through grace to discover the riches and beauty of the gospel. It isn't wrong to ask God to relieve you of your pain, but it is more important that in the midst of the pain you rely on the promise of God to work such experiences for his glory and your good—to use these times as a means of perfecting your faith, strengthening your spirit, and transforming your life in such a way that you are becoming more like Jesus.

I know you want relief, but often relief comes, not in the form of the removal of the affliction, but in the strengthening of your faith. And that is what these trials are designed to do—test, prove, and strengthen your faith. In times of ease you have sometimes wondered just how real and robust is your faith. In times of your own weakness you have asked

God to sanctify you, grow you, and strengthen you. Well, here is your answer. God accomplishes much of that through your "fiery trial" when you suffer well. To suffer well doesn't mean you put on a stoic face and muscle through the situation without a word. It means that through your suffering you trust God, bless him, look to him, and point others to him.

When the world strips away your comfort and confidence in things temporal, when friends become enemies and attack you, when in the providence of God suffering enters your life like a flash flood, you are given an opportunity to see very clearly where your ultimate dependence lies and where you find your identity. And it's not just something that reveals truth about yourself; it is also something God uses to sanctify you.

Do you want to be confident in God's good purposes for your life? Then you must discover them in times of ease as well as times of difficulty. Do you want to become more like Christ? Then you must suffer, and suffer well.

45
READ

Your testimonies are wonderful;
therefore my soul keeps them.
The unfolding of your words gives light;
it imparts understanding to the simple.
I open my mouth and pant,
because I long for your commandments.
Turn to me and be gracious to me,
as is your way with those who love your name.
Keep steady my steps according to your promise,
and let no iniquity get dominion over me.
Redeem me from man's oppression,
that I may keep your precepts.
Make your face shine upon your servant,
and teach me your statutes.
PSALM 119:129–135

Dear Self,
You need to stop looking at Scripture merely as a text to dissect and start reading it as God's Word given to you—today. Do you see how the psalmist thinks about God's Word? For him, Scripture is a wonder that imparts wisdom, and he is thirsty for it every day. Your default is to read to know, or to study to learn in less than practical, experiential ways. You are often interested in getting into the Word, but more as an

isolated discipline than the pursuit of God, and this robs you of the purpose of Scripture.

I'm not suggesting that you turn off your brain or ease up on continuing to learn how to deeply study Scripture. But what is clear is that Scripture requires both head and heart, and you need to see it not just as a text but as the very words of God. This will encourage you to pay close attention to the very words he uses, but it will also compel you to feast on those words as light-shedding, wisdom-dispensing, and life-giving counsel from on high.

For all of your longing for God to speak, to make his will plain and his plan clear, you should be daily immersed in God's Word. That is his voice, his will, and his plan made known to you. Consider these words, "Make your face shine upon your servant, and teach me your statutes." God's face shines on you when you are learning—experientially—his Word. This means his favor and blessing are upon you, and that you have sweet communion with him through Scripture, but only when you receive it for what it is: God's life-giving Word meant to be believed, received, and obeyed—not only dissected.

46

LIVE CAREFULLY

Look carefully then how you walk, not as unwise but as wise,
making the best use of the time, because the days are evil.

EPHESIANS 5:15–16

Dear Self,

You often presume upon God's grace and live recklessly. Better men than you have fallen hard by doing so. Believing that God is sovereign, that he causes all things to work together for your good, and that he is your hope of perseverance does not excuse or make allowance for reckless living. You? Live recklessly? Absolutely.

You live recklessly when you do not take God's law seriously or respond to the gospel properly. Reckless living can look like laziness and apathy. When you simply aren't motivated and tell yourself that God has forgiven you in Jesus, so you're not going to fight temptation and sin—that is reckless living, and it's far more dangerous than you realize. Reckless living is also giving yourself a pass on sin and moving into questionable practices without sufficient thought, or it's even indulging in sin, again assuring yourself that with Jesus as a Savior, you are secure in him.

When you dismiss the law, claiming Jesus has fulfilled it for you, without desiring to keep the law for the glory of God, you demonstrate a "faith" that has short-circuited. It amounts to your using the gospel as an excuse to not concern yourself with sin. It is a presumption that stems from a superficial faith. This reckless living will lead to your ruin.

Paul tells you to live carefully. This means thoughtfully, intentionally, and according to the will of God revealed in Scripture. In the broadest sense it means that you make the most of the time you have by living according to your God-given purpose. This is important, not only because it is right, but also because the days are evil. The world, the flesh, and the Devil are working against that purpose for your life and seeking your ruin.

Careful living is the intentional use of your time for God's glory, the good of others, and your own progress in the faith. It is living for a purpose that takes both the end and the journey seriously.

47

TAKE RISKS

Now great crowds accompanied him,
and he turned and said to them,
"If anyone comes to me and does not hate his own
father and mother and wife and children and brothers and sisters,
yes, and even his own life, he cannot be my disciple.
Whoever does not bear his own cross and come after me
cannot be my disciple.
. . . So therefore, any one of you who does not renounce all
that he has cannot be my disciple."

LUKE 14:25–27, 33

Dear Self,

The gospel demands that you risk the loss of everything for the glory of God and the good of your neighbors. In fact, Jesus says this even more forcefully. To be his disciple you must renounce everything to follow him. It doesn't seem like this has been your attitude regarding Jesus and the things of this life.

You know that salvation is of grace and that you receive it by faith alone. But faith in Jesus is not simple agreement with his words in principle; it is dependence on him to such a degree that you renounce all other things in life that have occupied a place of supremacy. And when Jesus really does come first, life becomes filled with risks. You risk the loss of family, reputation, prosperity, and more—for the world is hostile to this kind of allegiance and worship and hates the renunciation of those things the world loves to worship.

Jesus says you must consider the cost of being a disciple and then see if you have what it takes. This isn't a question about how strong you are, or how committed you can be, but whether your faith is legit. He says if you embark on this journey of following him and do not have faith, you will fail because you will not be able to let "goods and kindred" or "this mortal life" go when it comes down to choosing between them or Jesus. You can't make that kind of sacrifice apart from faith and the sustaining grace that comes from God.

Do you sense the risks that are involved in following Jesus? Are you aware? It's not just the world that will have trouble with your allegiance to Jesus. The religious crowd and maybe even some in the Christian community will challenge such radical allegiance. The question is, are you aware of the risks and ready to take them?

48

TAKE NOTE

Oh give thanks to the LORD; call upon his name;
make known his deeds among the peoples!
Sing to him; sing praises to him;
tell of all his wondrous works!
Glory in his holy name;
let the hearts of those who seek the LORD rejoice!
Seek the LORD and his strength;
seek his presence continually!
Remember the wondrous works that he has done,
his miracles and the judgments he uttered,
O offspring of Israel his servant,
sons of Jacob, his chosen ones!

1 CHRONICLES 16:8–13

Dear Self,

Like the Israel of old, you tend to forget the most basic things. Important things. You need constant reminders, and what you have been gleaning from others is not enough. You need to find ways to remind yourself about the things that matter, because when you aren't intentionally setting the truth before yourself you forget.

You forget that before you knew Jesus you were a slave to sin, a child of wrath, a dead man walking. And remembering these truths promotes humility in yourself and dependence on God. You forget that in Jesus you are his disciple, a child of God, a new creation. And remembering these truths creates gratitude and optimism. You forget that you are made for the glory of God and the good of your neighbors. And remembering these truths gives you purpose and passion. You forget that you're sent to make Christ known and to make disciples. And remembering these truths helps you see your need to be organically connected to the local church as well as the community God has sent you to.

Without reminders you will forget all of this and much more. And when you forget these things you get into trouble. This means you must do better than build a robust theology. You will have to exercise it. It demands setting that theology before yourself frequently. Israel erected "memorial stones" to remind themselves of the person and work of God. One of the primary ways you will remember the truth is by preaching it to yourself regularly. And keep in mind, it is only as you are preaching to yourself that you become truly ready to share these beautiful truths with others. You see, your spouse, your kids, and your friends need to be reminded as well.

And do you realize that you are doing it right now? You are reminding yourself of the need to preach to yourself, to remind yourself, and to not forget your God. Remember your God and his wonderful works.

RECOMMENDED READING

Christ Formed in You: The Power of the Gospel for Personal Change by Brian Hedges

The Cross Centered Life: Keeping the Gospel the Main Thing by C. J. Mahaney

Death by Love: Letters from the Cross by Mark Driscoll and Gerry Breshears

The Gospel for Real Life: Turn to the Liberating Power of the Cross . . . Every Day by Jerry Bridges

A Gospel Primer for Christians: Learning to See the Glories of God's Love by Milton Vincent

The Life of God in the Soul of Man by Henry Scougal

NOTES TO SELF

NOTES TO SELF

NOTES TO SELF

NOTES TO SELF

NOTES TO SELF

NOTES TO SELF